Praise for Maps Are Lines We Draw:

"Coffelt avoids the 'Haiti narrative' trap and instead takes us on a reflective and intellectual road trip. She's a natural at the fragmented essay form that builds and builds on small observations, all linked, all talking to each other. How lucky we are that Coffelt knew how to listen to all these whispers and collect them into this startling first book. Pick up this book if you've never read anything about Haiti or if you've read everything about Haiti: *Maps Are Lines We Draw* forges a new path."

—Jen Hirt, author of *Under Glass: The Girl with a Thousand Christmas Trees*

"Reflections that are steeped in humility like Ms. Coffelt's are rare and should be required reading for people pursuing short-term work in countries like Haiti."

—Joia Mukherjee
Department of Global Health and Social Medicine, Harvard University

"With her striking debut, Allison Coffelt weaves an eloquent collage of history and place, politics and policy, inquiry and knowledge. The lines that mark the boundaries between here and there are removed to reveal a complex Haiti, then redrawn to assemble an even more complex notion of aid. In these pages, Coffelt's steady gaze and sharp intellect guide and inform without faltering. There is a magnitude here, a rare ability to articulate a global empathy despite privileged origins, a stripping of the ego in order to embody the other. I'm certain her words will help us re-envision the world and reassess our individual positions in it for years to come."

—Angela Palm, author of *Riverine: A Memoir from Anywhere but Here*

"Early on in this thoughtful meditation, Coffelt remembers spinning a globe in her childhood room, allowing myriad representations of home and loss to pass beneath her fingers. Later, she muses, 'What is in the remnants?'—a fair question for any human being who longs to come to terms with history and complicity. Carefully researched and humbly told, Coffelt's memoir is a trip well worth taking."

—Joni Tevis, author of *The World Is On Fire: Scrap, Treasure, and Songs of Apocalypse*

"This book is an excellent ethics primer for any student, researcher, health care professional, volunteer, or just overall humanist who has been implicated in or is thinking of working in the context of development or relief work, with Haitians or elsewhere. *Maps Are Lines We Draw* is a definite required read for our midwifery students!"

—Kirsty Bourret, SF, MHSC
Départment Profession de Sage-femme
Université Laurentienne, Canada

"Coffelt has captured not just the essence of Haiti—its strong and warm people, vibrant culture, and painful yet triumphant history—but also the truth of charitable work in Haiti, including the pitfalls and often unfortunately sordid past. Mostly, though, I enjoyed her story because of the multiple perspectives she conveys throughout the book and the insights she shares as they occurred to her during this very personal journey of discovery—those 'Aha' moments—not of exciting discovery but dawning awareness."

—Jim Grant, Executive Director, Global
Birthing Home Foundation
Sponsor of Maison de Naissance Birth Center

"This book begins with another book—one Allison Coffelt read in her youth, which sketched the formlines of a country inside her and inspired the journey this book recounts so vividly. Across this compassionate and beautiful work, our narrator attempts to reconcile the 'nearly irreconcilable' difference between here and there. It made me wonder: Where in the world might readers of this book end up one day?"

—Ryan Van Meter, author of *If You Knew Now What I Knew Then*

"I have read many books on Haiti, but *Maps Are Lines We Draw* is something different. It is a wonderful book and a remarkable work. I recommend all my friends and colleagues read this book."

—Dr. Jean Gardy Marius, Founder, Oganizasyon Sante Popilè (OSAPO)

Maps Are Lines We Draw

Allison Coffelt

LANTERNFISH PRESS
PHILADELPHIA, PA

LANTERNFISH PRESS
399 Market St, Suite 360
Philadelphia, PA 19106
lanternfishpress.com

Cover Art
Design by Michael Norcross.
Image by Allison Coffelt.

Printed in the United States of America.
Library of Congress Control Number: 2017958989
ISBN: 9781941360149

With thanks to my many teachers.

One

Before the car ride, I am nervous.

Dr. Jean Gardy Marius, a friend of a friend, will pick me up from the southern city of Les Cayes to drive to his clinic, north of Port-au-Prince. We haven't met. I know he speaks some English; I don't know how much.

I am in Haiti after a decade of dreaming about Haiti. Once I was fifteen and a book came at the right time, and I fell in love with a place I'd never been.

Ten years later I am here, with a notebook, a tape recorder, my ears, my eyes, my touch. I am here in my body, in this *here* that was once *there*.

T/here.

I am here for myself, really, to keep learning how much I don't know.

I have just spent a little over a week in a birthing home called Maison de Naissance, a clinic for maternal and infant care, run by nurses and midwives. My trip with

Dr. Marius—Gardy, as he says to call him—will take two days. It comes in the middle of my eighteen days here. We'll go up Highway 2 until the capital, and the traffic will make a two-and-a-half-hour drive last almost five. After a night in Port-au-Prince, Gardy and I will ride up along the Caribbean Sea to his clinic in Rousseau.

Before Haiti—before most things, really—I would kneel before the globe in my childhood home and spin it. The globe was one of my favorite pastimes. My right hand traced waves along its bumpy skin at a frequency that always changed.

Wherever it lands, I would say, *is where I'll live when I grow up.*

My parents remember it differently: *This is where we'll live someday.*

Gardy speaks English well. He also knows Creole, French, Spanish, and German. He learned Creole, French, and English growing up in Haiti; Spanish during medical school in the Dominican Republic; and German when he met his wife, a German aid worker.

"It's good to learn languages when you're young," he says. "You can do it now. For me, I'm getting older, I sometimes mix them up."

Gardy is just reaching his mid-forties. He shaves his head. His lower jaw juts out a touch from his oval face and his serious expression melts when he sees someone he knows, which happens everywhere.

A slanted scar reaches across the right half of his

forehead. Whenever I see him, he wears dark-wash jeans and either a navy T-shirt with the name of his clinic, OSAPO, or a button-down dress shirt.

Gardy picks me up at the boarding house for the Brenda Strafford Hospital, where I've rented a room—the closest accommodations I could find to the birthing home miles out of town. The doctor who stays above me watches TV in the common room in the evenings, across the courtyard from his patients. I hang around the doorway of the kitchen with another *blan* visiting Maison de Naissance from the States. We talk to the cooks in snippets and one day ask to learn what they're making.

Under the sink, bathed in yellow light, a fish the size of my forearm rests in a bucket of water. Soon, oil will sizzle and two dull knives, one small and one big, will go to work on everything.

The first few nights we were here, the head cook made what she thought Americans would want: casserole. After a while, we coaxed her into serving Haitian food.

To crush garlic with a mortar and pestle: first, drop in one fresh clove. The younger cook demonstrates. Next, mash. She slides the heavy basin over. Your turn. It is in fact that simple, but my chunk of garlic leaps, arcing over the edge of the bowl. Pick it up from the countertop, toss it back in.

We are working with pieces and the way they collide with what's around them: force, pressure, heat. This collision is messy.

*

In the globe-spinning game, I was often fated to live in the ocean. When I tired of the sea, I would play again, pressing down as a continent or little island came whirling toward me to engineer a stop. I knew this was cheating—so I would turn it again and again, until the only sensation I could remember was my gridded fingertip skimming ridges and grooves of color.

Even then, I was beginning to recognize the happenstance of birth, the luck of geography, and the ease with which some people are able to move. You can't always choose your place. And I knew this.

As Gardy and I curve northeast toward the mountains, I tell him I spent the day before in Port-Salut. He says it's one of the best beaches in Haiti.

Kirsty, the director of the birthing home, and her husband, Mackenzie, had piled nine people into their Nissan Pathfinder and driven an hour southwest to the public beach. We rolled the windows down and sat toddlers in laps as our ears popped with the steep climbs and quick descents.

There is nothing like the sound of waves. The closest thing is pressing your ear against a conch for that quiet roar. At the beach with Kirsty and Mackenzie, cerulean water brushed fine white sand. Tables and chairs sat near the fringe. A guitarist and a group of singers played for tips. Atop a concrete slab, vendors sold souvenirs.

I kicked a soccer ball in the surf with young boys and

squeezed lemon over garlic-covered fish. I felt for bones between my teeth. My Prestige, the Haitian "American-style lager," sweated onto the red checkered tablecloth as I swam from shore and floated in warm waves that cradled and rocked my body.

Relax, my translator had told me, is a saying. "*Relax* in Haiti means everything is fine, everything is good."

"Port-Salut was great," I tell Gardy. "It was beautiful."

Beautiful here means beautiful, and stands in for all I don't know how to say. It describes the place, yes, but it's too sweeping. It's what people say by way of conclusion. Haiti is beautiful, but it's more than that; it's harder than that.

When I was with Kirsty and Mackenzie, who took me to the beach, I was comfortable in my language. They spoke Creole, French, and English.

When I played with their nieces and nephews, my Creole could have belonged to someone younger than the girl I hoisted above the sea. Her swimsuit's print was American stars and stripes; bright orange water wings hugged her arms. She giggled as she fell back into the water and got ready to go again. Beads dangled from her braids. I said *okay* and splashed to play, lacking other words. In this game, the water, wind, and waves muffled my muteness.

"Have you been to Île-à-Vache?" Gardy asks.

"The island south of here? I wanted to go, but the ferry

timing didn't work out."

"You have to go. It's so beautiful. It's the most beautiful." Gardy is shaking his head, grinning, squinting. Convincing me.

"When I come back," I say.

"Yes, you'll have to."

Gardy's mind travels south and hops the ferry—ocean, wind, and salt—while we head north to Port-au-Prince— concrete, crowds, and trapped heat.

I come back to language. The unspoken and the spoken trace lines and slide between us, like my finger atop the globe.

In Creole, I trip over words. I think in English. There was a time when I lived in Costa Rica, after a decade of study, that I finally began to think in Spanish.

I remember my host mother calling for me from the door, telling me we were late.

"¡Ya voy!" I said.

And she was before me, rocking on the balls of her feet, her narrow arms reaching out for my shoulders.

"¡Ya voy!" she repeated.

Ya voy is how you say I'm coming! It was common slang I'd picked up from her, not a book or the classroom. But its direct translation is "already I go," conflating my departure from here with my arrival there. Yes, I am coming: I am already on the way.

My host mother said I was like a native speaker now. She was so proud.

Sentence structure, whether learned automatically or deliberately, informs the way I think. The form of the possessive is inseparable from possession. In another language, the emphasis changes.

Grammar reflects the process of my mind.

Vocabulary is based in history.

When it comes to recording Haiti, foreigners typically speak English or French. So do the Haitian elite. These are the languages of gilded tongues, the privileged ones who tell the story loudest. Haiti's two official languages are French and Creole. They are listed in that order. But if French is learned at all, it's not the first language of most Haitians.

Haitian Creole is classified as a "patois," literally "rough speech," and embodies a divide. It's a dialect rooted in class, seen by some as bastardized French and not its own pure language. But what language can be pure, really?

The French half of the island of Hispaniola, Saint-Domingue, was crucial in the Atlantic slave trade. Slave labor drove the colony that would be Haiti to become the world's biggest producer of coffee and supply 75 percent of the globe's sugar.[1] This from a place the size of Maryland.

Creole was raised between sugarcane and slaves, blending West African languages and everyday French. It was born out of a desire for solidarity, the need for communication, and a longing for freedom.

*

Ayiti, as it is spelled in Creole, comes from the Arawak language of the Taíno people who were here before the Europeans and those the Europeans enslaved. It means "land of the mountains."[2]

As Gardy and I wind around these mountains, I ask, "You grew up in Les Cayes?"

"Yes, I was born here and lived here for a while."

"Then where did you go?"

"It's a long story."

Gardy and I are riding the edge of the mountains. The road folds in and out over the ridges.

"Well," I say, pausing. "We have a long drive." I change my mind. "But if you don't feel like it, I understand."

He drives with his left hand wheeling between ten and two, right hand resting on the stick. Outside our windows, flashes of bright green leaves—here, the fernlike branches and long, thin seed pods of the lead tree—burst from red dirt.

We are not yet far from the ocean. When we hit a straightaway, clear and—there's no other word for it—*sparkling* blue water finds my eyes. It almost hurts in its intensity, but I keep looking. I pick at the Land Cruiser's grooved grey leather bench. Gardy begins his story.

There's comfort in the couch: you can look straight out, yet feel another's weight. It's an audience without a gaze.

Gardy was born in Les Cayes in 1969. As we drive by his mother's house, he points it out. It's salmon pink, and

I turn my head back after we've passed, saying, "That one?" A clothesline is strung off to the side. There are four, maybe five rooms, which makes it bigger than many homes I've seen in the area. It was not the house where Gardy grew up.

Gardy's father left his mother not long after he was born. When he was five, his mother remarried.

"My stepfather was always drinking alcohol," Gardy says. "He would beat my mother, and beat my sister. He hated having me in the house because I did not belong to him. I was not his son.

"In Haiti, culturally, when you are the oldest, the responsibility is always on your shoulders. So you are the man, and you have to take responsibility. I could not say, 'Hey, it's over, stop beating my mother. Stop treating her like nothing.' Because I was too little. I was so powerless.

"You get to the point, and you say, well, your house is burning and you have the choice. Stay in the house, you're going to die. Maybe you know going outside is another risk, but you have a little opportunity to survive. I got to that point, and I said, well, I need to take an action. So that's what I did. But I knew—if I fail, he's going to kill me."

Gardy was twelve at the time.

"I did not fail with my action. I hit him very deeply with a big bottle, so when they took him to the hospital, he was confused. I had the feeling that it was my last time in the house because—I knew. If he came back home, I wouldn't be able to stay there. I had to go away."

Gardy and his mother had to make a quick decision.

He had an uncle and a cousin in Port-au-Prince. He'd go.

"But at the same time, it was so painful, because—what's going to happen with my brothers and sisters? What's going to happen with my mom?

"It was so difficult. It was. But I am proud that at that age I had enough courage to take action and show him that I did not agree with him and the way he treated us—treated my mother, and brothers and sisters, in the house.

"Where I am today is a result of my action. Maybe if I stayed home, life would be completely different. It was a long way to go from leaving my house to being here today. A long way. A long, difficult way."

What does it mean to keep a globe in your home? That the world is yours? That your parents are educated? That the beauty of thin lines does not escape you?

That you have the means for geographic curiosity.

To be *here for myself, really, to keep learning how much I don't know.* The privilege to pursue a collision that will be inescapably uncomfortable. At best, awkward. At worst, culpable. Likely both.

A Haitian maxim: The rock in the water does not know the pain of the rock in the sun.

Now I carry a map, that two-dimensional collage of lines, on a telephone in my pocket. I can zoom out and see the whole world laid flat. This may be a regression in thinking, or it might be truer than ever. But I know this: a map is not a globe; it has no tilt; you cannot run your fingers along its curve or spin it until the lines and words are all a blur.

*

Driving up Highway 2, I picture Gardy at twelve years old, fleeing home. Maybe he's wearing his school uniform—navy shorts and a white dress shirt—because it's the nicest thing he owns and he hopes to start school again at his uncle's house. Maybe he carries a small bag with a few bills from his mother buried inside. He's headed for the big city, where supposedly there are jobs. Certainly there will be changes.

Gardy takes this same route now, decades and hundreds of trips after that first time, and still we rewind. The roadside whizzes by through the glass. We are going back.

Two

When Gardy asks why I'm in Haiti, I fumble. He is really asking about guides, about how a white woman from Missouri ended up sharing his front seat.

The first guide might be these mountains, and how ten years ago I came to them through the page and cannot forget them.

Here is how I almost said it: *These mountains, and how they came to me.*

But they were first. We are here because of what is there.[1]

The book that introduced me to Haiti, Tracy Kidder's *Mountains Beyond Mountains*, came from guide two: my favorite teacher, who taught global health to high-school students through stories. I took his class at a time when sincerity was social suicide. It was cool not to care, but I—and more likely we, so many of his students—longed to be part of something bigger than ourselves.

Mountains Beyond Mountains came at a moment when I was open to being changed, and so it altered my trajectory. The book followed the story of Dr. Paul Farmer and his organization Partners In Health as they worked in Haiti to exercise a "preferential option for the poor."[2] It was a philosophy that says poor people, too, have the right to quality health care, among other things.

As we drive, Gardy and I survey the roadside fruit stands. Fruit in the city can't compare to fruit from the country in cost or in quality. Mountain fruit is juicy and not long off its vine. We come upon a group of women under a tarp and slow down. Gardy observes the bowls of sugar apples—*cashima*; they look like big artichokes with softer spikes—and baskets of flat green peas, and accelerates again. We pass other merchants without acknowledgment.

From the 2011 Lonely Planet guide to the Dominican Republic and Haiti: "Today's travelers are reminded of the French Riviera as they approach the Haitian capital from the west. Silhouetted against a crescent of wooded mountains, the shining white city faces the emerald-cobalt Gulf of Gonâve."[3]

I ask Gardy what he's looking for; he shrugs and says he wants the right stand. As the truck climbs another peak, Gardy sees several women sitting together, opposite us, and pulls over.

*

The first written record of the word *guide* came in 1362 from poet William Langland. A *gyde* keeps him safe from something *wicked*.[4]

My paperback copy of *Mountains* feels lighter than I remember. A small square of notebook paper nestled into the spine on page 109 says *amenazar* and, on the flip side, *to threaten*. An old Spanish flashcard. The browning pages and old-book smell challenge the feeling that I only just read it. This book has moved with me nine or ten times, at least. It was packed on a summer spent in Boston, working for the organization I'd idolized.

I remember sitting at lunch in a Chinese market. I was twenty-one.

"Do you see yourself working on the ground, or do you think you'll do the kind of development work—fundraising—that you're doing now?" the Partners In Health staffer asked.

I said I didn't know.

"Definitely on the ground," said the intern next to me.

I said I didn't know.

"Yeah," the staffer said, "on the ground is where it's at."

Maybe a guide keeps you physically safe—but what of other wickedness?

The danger of the mission-trip story. The college-admittance or finding-God experience. You know the one: a student goes somewhere "down there," and as soon as she gets off the plane ("it was really hot") they take a bus to the village, and they meet locals and maybe teach some children English, and at the end of the week, that glorious week, when all this time she thought she would be teaching them, she really finds *they* taught her. A tale so common I once heard a radio interview about just how common it is.[5]

I'm not sure knowing this trap gets me out of it.

I'm not sure I'm so different.

Back at the St. Louis airport, there had been a group of young people, maybe fourteen or fifteen years old, in bright yellow T-shirts waiting to board. One of the chaperones, a man in his mid-forties, had leaned over to me.

"We're going to Haiti," he said.

His lanyard read *Illinois State Baptist Association.* He asked where I was from. When I told him Columbia, Missouri, he asked if I knew the First Baptist Church there. I said I used to live near it.

The man and I exchanged strangers-in-an-airport talk. We'd both driven hours to get to this first flight. We'd both have an overnight in Miami. His group would be helping at an orphanage, one impacted by the earthquake. He traveled a lot for his job, he said, but never outside the United States—well, except Canada, if you can count Canada. I count Canada, I said. Okay then, Canada. But when he'd gone there, you could just drive across the border, no papers needed. So you had to get a passport for this trip, I said, and he nodded and told me he'd had to go to the post office.

I pictured him in line to get his passport and I softened. I wanted so badly—maybe still want—to draw a line between myself and this man. Me *here*; him *there.* Maybe at the post office he tells the guy behind him where he's going and gets a nod, which is all the encouragement he needs to say more. My own first time in that passport line had been a decade ago. I'd stood on the X between the camera and the white projector screen and felt like I could go anywhere. It was as if the world, after I left that grey building, became bigger and smaller at the same time.

In his historical analysis of travel writing, James Buzard highlights a pattern of the self-interrupting form. It is part of a larger distinction between *traveler* and *tourist*, a label difference that hinges largely on *perceived* authenticity.

Apparently, "it became an expected feature" for travel writers to separate themselves from "tourist-serving institutions . . . by self-consciously demonstrating independence from them."[6]

The desire to separate is not a new one.

The women on the roadside gather their fruit bowls—as much as they can carry—from under the tarp canopies and rush to the truck. Gardy leaves it idling and hops out to meet them. We conduct business at the back of the truck: him teasing the women, them protesting back.

Oh no, no, chérie, he sweet-talks.

"I love the haggle," he says later, "but I always want to pay a fair price."

Gardy says he sees his mother in the women he meets at the fruit stand.

*

From the 1956 Pan Am brochure "Visit Haiti": "Haiti's brilliant hues are tempered with deeper tones, both in nature and human types. One sees them in the depths of shaded coffee groves, in the mountains darkly purple at dusk, in polished mahogany and rosewood pieces. In ebony skins of peasants, descended from African chieftains, in the *café-au-lait* complexions of the mulatto minority."[7]

A cattle egret hovers, flapping, and lands on the shoulder of a cow near the roadside. It catches bugs while the cow grazes. Breakfast for two.

The animals in Haiti are skinny. A couple of mutts hang around the boarding house in Les Cayes where I've been staying. The female is chestnut-brown with a dark spot near her eye and floppy ears. She won't let you touch her. The other is lighter, taupe-brown, and a little rounder. It's hard to tell their ages.

The cows in the fields here look like the dogs: too skinny to be cows. They lope through the fields with visible rib cages, protruding haunches, and tails switching back and forth. Many of them drag a rope, a leash, from their necks.

I am from the Midwest, where we hold dear the memory of stockyards and cattle cars, the myth of the good old days. We cook barbecue and drink milk with supper. No matter if our fields are now full of soybeans and corn that people cannot eat; the identity holds. It is the story we tell about ourselves.

*

Guides three, four, five, and six might be places I've worked: organizations, internships, jobs. Missouri, Massachusetts, California, back again to Missouri. Organizing for Maison de Naissance in college, interning for Partners In Health in Boston, student organizing in California, a job at a nonprofit in my hometown. Each time, wondering: Does it matter? To whom?

I saw things and was seen, and for a while my only response was to separate. I could boycott brands; I could direct my anger at capitalism. I funneled rage into political organizing. I wanted to be separate from the system that had allowed—thrived—on the suffering I was awakening to. When you are part of the system you want to examine, how do you step far enough away to hold it up to the light?

"The goofiness of radicals thinking they have to dress in Guatemalan peasant clothes. The poor don't want you to look like them. They want you to dress in a suit and go get them food and water."[8] This quote from Paul Farmer in *Mountains Beyond Mountains* would bounce in my head for years after I read it.

Gardy and I have progressed to the next stage of fruit selection.

"Pineapple?"

"Yes, we want pineapple."

"How about this?"

A woman offers Gardy a small green ball.

"Here, let me try," he says.

He takes his knife from his pocket and peels back its

light lime skin.

"Have you tried this before? It's an orange."

A green orange. I bite. Gardy laughs at my pucker. This green orange is made of pulpy nodules, but it's far from sweet. He takes a chunk for himself and buys a few to go with us.

Gardy is guide seven—lucky seven, holy seven—but this count is arbitrary, after all. He just as well could have been guide number fifteen, or four.

We add tart cherries to our heap, to blend with sugar for juice. Starfruit goes in, too. So does cantaloupe. Oranges, papaya. Gardy buys something from each woman.

The fruit rests in the bed of the Land Cruiser between sugarcane stalks, given to Gardy by his mother, and a few bags. When we take off, the melons start moving. I twist around to fix them.

"Don't worry about it. Don't worry, don't worry." Gardy says. "They're just going for a ride. But they can't get out."

"Sugarcane is native of the plains, where the traveller often sees, with astonishment, gigantic specimens of it, varying from 18 to 24 feet in height," says the 1861 *Guide to Hayti*, whose goal was to inspire Black Americans, former slaves, to emigrate to the island.[9]

The sugarcanes in the back of the Land Cruiser are the size of good walking sticks. In Port-au-Prince I will see people in markets carving into these, selling off the wet, white meat in shards.

Mackenzie, Kirsty's husband, once took me and the

other *blan* to the public market near Maison de Naissance. Donkeys walked by, loaded with goods piled on wooden saddle trees. A merchant arranged her wares on a tarp: starfruit, eggplant, cherries, melons, and pineapples.

Women passed by holding one or two freshly killed chickens by the feet. One woman had a chicken dangling in each hand and a live turkey sitting in a basket on her head, unaware of his fate. His gobbler was loose and gangly, purplish grey.

I heard screaming. A small child throwing a tantrum. This was the first time, I realized, aside from the infants in the birthing home, that I'd heard children yelling in public. I looked around for the voice as the squealing grew angrier and more piercing. I didn't see a mother dragging a hand; I saw two men walking toward me with small, dark pigs in brown burlap sacks. They hoisted them up and the heads of the pigs peeked out of the sacks. Their squeals rose higher. In the livestock section of the market, you could buy a goat for about thirty US dollars. I'm not sure about a piglet.

Mackenzie saw me watching as people hopped into the bed of a *tap-tap*, a brightly painted taxi truck. Two men had begun to string together the front and back feet of their newly bought lambs and loop the rope over the top of the truck bed, near the right back wheel. The lambs, upside down, hung like a woman's purse from her shoulder.

"It's very bad," Mackenzie said, "the way we treat animals here in Haiti. Very bad. It's hard to see it."

I pictured the lambs on the way home as the driver

shifted and braked, swinging as he accelerated and bumping as he changed lanes. At that moment, though, they just blinked big black eyes set in narrow, curly-fleeced heads. Their stumpy tails couldn't fight gravity so they hung upside down, exposed.

The word *travel* comes from *travail*, as in "bodily or mental labor or toil, especially of a painful or oppressive nature."[10]

In other words: work, for both mind and body.

Three

"Come on out, *chérie!*" Louna Julien called in Creole through the curtain door.

This was back at Maison de Naissance, where Louna is a community health promoter. She walks door to door and counsels people about health practice; we were at the sixth home of the day and would go to at least six more. At that moment she was talking Altidor Lucienne back out onto the porch for a picture—Altidor had agreed to a photo, then asked us to wait. She reemerged dressed up, in a denim skirt and black tank top. She was holding a comb.

"You look great," Louna said. "Come on! Let's take it!"

At each home, Louna speaks to the woman or the man or sometimes the children. She talks, depending on her audience, about the birthing home's HIV services, about breastfeeding, family planning, or how to clean water. Altidor has two young sons, Julien and Carlos, so their conversation centered on breastfeeding and family planning, though they touched on a little of everything.

Altidor's home was set back from the road on a concrete slab, the lower half painted a copper color and the upper half a muted yellow. The trim was turquoise. A clothesline zagged from the peak of the roof to a nearby palm tree; her little boys' underwear dangled like prayer flags.

As I stepped back with my camera, they looked at me and smiled, and then I asked them to face each other and reenact their conversation. There's something about this staging that is both a surprise and a comfort: the costume change, the choice of what to put in the frame.

The shutter clicked.

At the end of my day with Louna, she asked if I'd like to see her house. "It's right over there," she said, gesturing beyond a line of trees. I said, "Of course," and we walked with my interpreter pushing his motorbike, following her directions. She paused to buy rolls, the bread white and gummy, from a walking seller and, further up the mostly empty gravel road, called to a woman balancing a bucket atop her head. They met and Louna exchanged coins for ice pops. "The children love these," she said.

The children—including nieces and nephews—sat with Louna's sister on the porch as we approached. The home had maybe a foot of foundation, with grey river rocks stacked along the side for landscaping. It had smooth floors, windows, and four or five rooms; it was one of the nicest houses I'd seen. I met her family, and when Louna asked if I would like anything, I asked to use her bathroom.

"Okay?" I ask.

"Okay."

She led me around the left side of the house and into the backyard, where clothes hung from the line. In the far right corner was a small, roofless structure made of cement blocks. A seat-height tower of the same rough bricks emptied into a hole far below. There was no door, just a fourth wall that didn't quite meet the corner.

Louna called to her children to bring *papier*. One returned with a roll and handed it to me.

"*Mèsi.*"

She told them to bring a swatch of tin from the yard; they pulled over what looked like a piece from an old roof. I walked in; she leaned the metal against the gap in the wall. I squatted.

There was a gust of wind. There was a gust of wind because of *course* there was a gust of wind.

The door fell, and Louna was there with her children. I looked at them.

They looked at me looking at them.

My mouth must have been a bit agape. I held my *papier* in my right hand, which was the only side of me they could see. Louna snapped to action.

"No, no, no." She swiveled her daughter out of the way, grabbed the makeshift door, and propped it up again. She held it to the wall like a guard on patrol.

"*Mèsi!*" I said.

I zipped up and pressed lightly on the door to get out. "Okay!" I called. She held firm. I pressed another time. Then lightly knocked and yelled, "Okay! *Mèsi!*" She released me and, as we headed up front, she handed me a small plastic bottle.

"Clorox," Louna said. She flipped up the lid of the unlabeled bottle and squirted some diluted bleach on my hands. She mimed hand-washing and I followed suit, flicking drops from my wrist. It was the liquid I'd heard her explain at every house—discussing different strengths for the floor, countertops, water vessels, and hand-washing with the patients she met.

—Do you know how to keep your water clean?

I heard this question, and the conversations around it, both out in the field and back at the birthing home.

*—I will wait two days to bring home my son
and five months before I sell rice again.*

We often use the terms *translator* and *interpreter* interchangeably.

*—One pill will clean three small
bottles, the size of Coca-Cola.*

*—She hemorrhaged during the birth
and almost bled to death.*

*—The water treatment takes half an hour. If you don't
have a watch, that means wait for a good moment.
It's the time it takes to walk from here to the road.*

*

There is a difference: *translation* means written;[1] *interpreting* refers to the spoken word.[2] A translator renders text—words already set down. An interpreter conveys language as it forms and meanings as they're made.

> —*Her husband is back at work today.*

The adage, "there's room for interpretation."

> —*You wash your hands, your dishes, with Clorox.*

The adage, "a good translator disappears."

> —*I buy the rice from the farm. We boil it. After that, we dry it in the sun and go to a grinder to grind and clean it. Then we sell it in a public market.*

> —*Why are you a nurse?*
> —*I love the community, and I want to help people and also help my family.*

> —*I don't have any other activities. This way, I can do something to make an impact.*

"Haiti: More than Just Rubble." From the 2011 *Lonely Planet* guide.[3]

> —*What would you change?*
> —*Health care for our families, better roads, lower*

cost of schools, fewer injustices in the legal system.

—At the time, we were eating at the table. She was talking with me and said, "I felt something bite me."

—It's hard, but I do it because I can't do anything else.

—And she fell. And died.
—She left a baby: three months, ten days.

—I build cabinets. I am a cabinet maker. I want to work.

"The Haitians are a happy people." From the 1956 *Pan Am* brochure.[4]

—Sometimes my son says, "When will Mommy come back?"

—I am strong. I want to work.

—Life is like that. Nobody can prevent death from coming into your home.

—Will you remember my story?

Four

After Gardy moved into his uncle's house in Port-au-Prince, he planned to re-enroll and attend school with his cousins. He turned to his uncle for help with school fees, but his uncle put him to work in the house.

Laundry, cooking, cleaning, repairs, errands. Gardy would walk his cousins to school every day and return home to work. I imagine him laundering uniforms and packing lunches, hoping his turn would come.

Gardy and I drive up Highway 2, which follows the Canal de la Gonâve and eventually meets the Caribbean Sea, then the Atlantic. Before this road turns to follow the coast, however, it cuts across Haiti's peninsula. From Les Cayes to the major port of Miragoâne is just over a hundred kilometers.

We pass a small town, and through the window I see a man whose shirt implores, *SAVE SENIOR WEEK*. A few days ago I walked by someone wearing the grey, red-lettered *D.A.R.E.* shirt from my middle school's "Just Say No to Drugs" program.

I have seen stock footage of women in vivid oranges and reds, perhaps with head wraps of majestic purple, carrying pitchers of water on their crowns. But this is not how Haiti is.

Haiti is a graveyard for clothes.

From the raw materials stage, US cotton subsidies guarantee a hefty price for cotton from American growers—while increasing the global supply and driving down the world market price. Though opinion pieces, individual politicians, and even two US presidents have argued against such steep subsidies, legislation in the last decade has included not just safety nets but payouts. "Growers," writes Pietra Rivoli, "can now opt for protection against declines in revenue from falling crop yields."[1]

An artist friend once told me of a color trend that reflects a society's "development." According to this theory, women in poorer countries tend to embrace bold colors and bright hues more than women in richer countries. The latter prefer more subtle shades and neutrals. *Developed, developing.*

I've read about language as a boomerang—the words chosen say more about the speaker than about what they describe.

I cannot find anything about this color trend when I look, and I wonder if I'm misremembering. Could it be that paler-skinned women tend to prefer neutrals? That, really, any such trend reflects which colors enhance the complexions of those who have historically been the exploiters?

I do not own many bright shades.

First World, Third World, industrialized, rising.

What *we* call *them.*

The term *Third World* is a holdover from the Cold War, when the US and its allies saw themselves as the First World. The Soviet-bloc countries were considered "second," and all the other places, many of which were formerly colonies, were "third."[2]

Back in Les Cayes, merchant stations lined the streets. Driving to the birthing home on weekdays, we passed stations selling produce, hair barrettes, soccer balls, crackers, and—especially—clothes. Prom dresses hung from eight-foot-high concrete embankments. Stiff blue ruffles and shiny maroon rayon flashed as we rounded corners. There were cotton dresses, collared shirts, and tank tops, too, but mostly there were T-shirts.

Creole has a word for these imported castoffs: *pèpè.*

There were in fact pitchers of water to be carried, and sometimes baskets. Even chairs might be balanced atop a woman's head. Picture this—then picture that woman getting on a motorbike. She is wearing *pèpè.*

Between 1990 and 2007, 9 billion pounds of used

textiles were exported from America to other countries, Rivoli reports.[3] They are purchased by companies like Trans-Americas Trading Company to be sorted, packaged, shipped, and sold in huge bundles to places like Haiti.

Places like Haiti.

Other places have created a vocabulary around this Goodwill fashion show.

In Tanzania, secondhand imports are *mitumba*.[4]

Bolivia: *ropa usada*.

They are known in Zambia as *salable*.

For two years, Gardy worked for his uncle. "The only hope I had when I decided to go to my uncle was that he was going to help me go to school. So by the time I realized he was using me like a servant in his house— he never showed any interest in me going to school—I decided to leave."

He was fourteen years old.

I picture him walking alongside the stations of merchandise.

"We slept in the streets, we ate in the streets, we lived in the streets."

It is the first time I hear Gardy say it, but he will invoke the same refrain every time he tells this story.

We slept in the streets, we ate in the streets, we lived in the streets.

Sometimes he says it in outrage, sometimes imploringly; other times it seems a challenge for you to look at him now, know his history, and see Haiti as a place where transformation can abide.

"This was one of my, I would say, one of the hardest moments in my life," Gardy says.

In Port-au-Prince, he got by with help from a group of young homeless boys. There were groups who would scrounge for food together, find work as day laborers, and scout out places to sleep.

"I remember we used to sleep in groups. Maybe we were in the street, sleeping, and some guy came back from the club. He was drunk, and he was peeing in the street, and he would pee on us.

"And sometimes, when you live in the street, you have to beg—begging people who drive by in cars. People tell you things you'd never expect to hear from them. They spit in your face.

"But you had to ask, because you needed something to eat. You had no choice, you had nothing else to do and no place to go. You had to do all of this."

Gardy remembers the people he knew then; remembers sharing water and food with one of his friends who had tuberculosis.

"I was so fortunate to leave without any kind of diseases or infection."

I met Nancie Wayack, a merchant, as she sat on a concrete bench under the birthing home's *choukounet*: a thatch-roofed gazebo, both meeting place and waiting room. She was waiting for her pregnant friend, who was inside at an appointment. Nancie sells clothes and food. To get goods to sell, she pays a car to take her up this highway Gardy and I are traveling, and goes to the warehouse in Miragoâne.

Trans-Americas Trading Company has been "recycling textiles since 1942" and calls itself an "innovator and an industry leader." The company pays "reputable charities millions of dollars annually for their unwanted clothing."[5] It sorts, compresses, packs, and seals clothing; 54,000 pounds goes into every forty-foot High-Cube Container.[6] Those shipping crates are then sent halfway across the globe.

Flooding markets is what we call it when a rush of goods enters the picture. Sudden supply makes whatever it is less valuable. Prices *plummet* like anchors searching for some kind of bottom.

We talk about markets, say they *rise* or *dry up* as if they're uncontrollable and rushing, the life force of water, and all there is to do is get out of the way.

Haitian businessmen with the green cards and paperwork to travel go to the United States and buy huge clothing shipments from vendors like Trans-Americas Trading Company. These businessmen bring their newly purchased bales to Haitian warehouses in Miragoâne and elsewhere. They're broken down and sold by weight.

Nancie's clothing comes by the bundle. She cannot choose the clothes. She sells what she gets and hopes it's enough to cover her children's school fees.

Nancie lives in a country with fewer than 1,500 public primary schools. There are 4 million people under the age of fifteen.[7] Even if the public schools and the population were spread evenly, there would be more than 26,000 students for each public school. This is why, so often, the only option is a parochial or private education.

On our way to Miragoâne, Gardy drives a time machine, his vision fixing on a younger self.

A friend of his in Port-au-Prince, one of the other young boys from the streets, was going back to his hometown, a small village called Rousseau, for the weekend. He asked Gardy if he wanted to come.

Until I saw Rousseau myself, I wouldn't understand why this boy had left his family. Thirty years after Gardy's first trip, it is still barely a town. Small clusters of one-room houses with dirt floors and thin mud walls line a few rocky roads.

The bustling capital, with its potential for food and jobs, had its allure.

When he was visiting Rousseau, Gardy and his friend joined a community game of soccer. After the match, a man approached him. Gardy was a new face in a small town.

"I told him I was living in Port-au-Prince. I told him I was working, because to say you are living on the streets—it's shameful."

Maybe this man had seen enough street kids to know it was a lie; maybe Gardy's limbs were too thin for the man to believe he had enough to eat.

"How about you stay here?" the man asked him. "I will give you a job. Work for me, and you can go to school."

"I saw young guys," Gardy says of his streetmates, "who maybe had more potential than I had, and they did not have the same opportunity, the same privilege I had—someone to get me from the street and put me in school. They got involved in drugs, they got sick, and contracted infections like HIV and died with tuberculosis. I never thought I would be able to get out of that situation, but I did."

The man who gave Gardy the job was Dr. Ronald Chalestin at Pierre Payen Hospital, not far from Rousseau. He put Gardy to work in the pharmacy. By age fifteen, Gardy was organizing medicine and helping fill orders. He was back in school and doing well.

"T-shirts made from Caribbean-made fabric using US-made yarn may enter the United States freely, but only to a limit of 5,651,520 dozen in 2003."[8] This sentence comes from Rivoli's reports on the 2002 US-Caribbean Trade Partnership Act. Note the detail: 5,651,520 dozen. This number is the maximum output of Fruit of the Loom factories in the United States. "This maneuver gave free access for the firm's T-shirt products into the United States while at the same time dissuading competitors from setting up rival T-shirt manufacturing plants in the Caribbean," writes Rivoli.[9]

In the years since this particularity, import regulations have been in constant flux. Lobbyists fight continually over definitions (is a collar on a shirt a "component" or a "trim"?) that determine what qualifies under which import tax.[10] To those advocating for fewer regulations, "the only thing more outrageous than all of these rules is to hear them [NAFTA, CBTPA, etc.] referred to as 'free trade' agreements."[11]

After about a year in the pharmacy, Dr. Chalestin asked Gardy if he wanted more responsibility. Did he want to assist in the rest of the hospital? Gardy would be at his side in the operating room. He would help hold tools, work with the tray, and follow orders from anyone in the room.

"It sounds crazy to someone from the US," Gardy says. It did. It does, still.

I used to purge my closet every few years. When a slow accumulation of stuff reached its height, it was time to go to Goodwill.

Then I would begin again: a bargain here, a clearance there, eventually cleaning it out. I told myself it was okay; I was donating.

One man's trash is another man's treasure.

Sometimes when I gave away piles of garments, I felt a rush of generosity. Other times, I felt the nagging guilt of waste.

Yarn-forward, fabric-forward, fiber-forward:[12] Was the yarn made *here* or the fabric and everything after? These terms are ways we draw lines, to say what makes something come from over *there*.

These rules are one way to navigate the rise and fall of market waters, to guide them like banks of a river. Their rise and fall is determined by people who have power—the people at the dam.

Gardy assisted with surgeries for another few years. Slowly, he earned more responsibilities. He began to assist Dr. Victor Binkley in surgery, where he was learning how to cut. The training was supervised and small, but Gardy was doing surgery. And he was excellent.

Confluence: "The act or process of merging," or the point where two rivers flow together.[13]

When Gardy was eighteen, Dr. Stuart Smith, a retired American doctor and a devout Christian on a medical mission trip, came to the hospital where he worked. Dr. Smith saw Gardy assist with a surgery.

"Are you in medical school?" he asked.

"No."

"Have you ever considered medical school?"

"No, I could never afford medical school."

"You showed more potential in that one surgery," he said, "than my US medical students. The most potential I have ever seen."

Dr. Smith got to know Gardy. When he returned home to Michigan, he kept thinking about how the young man might access medical school.

*

Is confluence inevitable? Is it by chance?
Can it be simultaneously *meant to be* and *lucky*?

The doctor saw only one way.

Dr. Smith had found in Gardy what he believed Haiti needed more of: a Haitian who could help his own country, if only he had the right resources. Dr. Smith had those resources. He came to a decision as part of his faith.

"He offered to pay for my medical school," Gardy says. "He used his life savings."

Five

When Dr. Smith made Gardy the offer, most Haitian medical students had been attending school in either the Dominican Republic or Cuba.

"But you have to realize," Gardy said, "the year was 1992."

"Oh," I said.

He waited.

"*Oh*," I said.

"Yes."

"The coup?"

"Exactly."

In 1990, Haiti held its first free and fair election since its war for independence ended in 1804.

In the three decades leading up to the election, Haiti had been under the reign of the Duvaliers. Papa Doc, as the former physician François Duvalier was called, named himself president for life and proved to be Haiti's most violent ruler. Somewhere between 30,000 and 60,000 people were killed during his presidency. His Tonton Macoute, a paramilitary force, killed or captured ordinary citizens. He divided Haiti into about 500 sections, drawing on the remnants of US Marine barracks and outposts left over from our twenty-year occupation of Haiti in the early twentieth century.[1] Then he appointed section chiefs whose job was to ensure submission to the government on every level.

When his son Jean-Claude Duvalier took over at the age of nineteen, the violence continued. Baby Doc's advisors played a larger role in decision-making but, still, opposition was not an option. During his fifteen years in power, he spent notorious amounts of money: his state-sponsored wedding cost $3 million.[2] When he eventually left office in the mid-1980s after uprisings, he fled to France. Military dictators fought over the presidency until the election of 1990.

The election was a confluence of forces.

Support had been growing for a populist party called Fanmi Lavalas among the poor. And after decades of removed import controls, the dismantling of labor unions, and the increased presence of foreign—especially US—corporations, there were a lot of poor people.

Lavalas translates to *flood* in Creole, or *mass of people* or *everyone together.*[3]

At the same time, a young priest named Jean-Bertrand Aristide practicing liberation theology in the slums of

Port-au-Prince was gaining popularity.

Liberation theology was popularized across Latin America by the Peruvian Catholic priest Gustavo Gutiérrez. "If there is no friendship with the poor and no sharing of the life of the poor, then there is no authentic commitment to liberation, because love exists only among equals," he writes.[4] It calls Christians to place service to the poor, as well as opposition to the structures that create poverty, at the center of their faith.

Father Aristide won the election on December 16, 1990, in a landslide. In a field of eleven candidates, Aristide earned more than two-thirds of the vote.[5]

From an interview with Jean-Bertrand Aristide in 2006:

"A student asked me: 'Father, do you think that by yourself you'll be able to change this situation, which is so corrupt and unjust?' And in reply I said: 'In order for it to rain, do you need one or many raindrops? In order to have a flood, do you need a trickle of water or a river in a spate?' . . . It is not alone, as isolated drops of water, that you or I are going to change the situation but together, as a flood or torrent, *lavalassement*, that we are going to change it, to clean things up, without any illusions that it will be easy or quick."[6]

During the first few months of his presidency, Aristide invited the poor to come eat on the lawn of the Presidential Palace.[7] The palace sits on a wide boulevard in the capital, and its lawn is vast and open against the packed, cramped city. "The palace is the center point around which all dreams of grandeur and all the nation's hopes collide," writes Dany Laferrière in his memoir of the earthquake. "People have never mistaken the building for its occupier."[8]

The soldiers, a force that had been used almost exclusively against Haiti's people by the Duvaliers, served them food on the lawn of this dream of grandeur.

Rice and beans, of course.[9]

On Aristide's inauguration day, he fired most of the top commanders in the military and began removing abusive section chiefs. The community would elect officials in their stead and a more neutral police force would be built. Aristide appointed a commission to investigate killings under the Duvaliers.

Aristide also opened up Fort Dimanche, the Duvaliers' torture chamber and the site of a massacre where soldiers had opened fire on protesters. The public could now visit the place where thousands of their loved ones had spent their last days.[10]

Policy changes under Aristide included finally collecting import fees and raising taxes on the wealthy. He began programs for improving adult literacy, redistributing fallow lands, and increasing enforcement of drug-trafficking laws. He worked to lower food prices and increase the minimum wage.[11]

"To set aside sympathy we extend to others beset by war and murderous politics," writes Susan Sontag, "for a reflection on how our privileges are located on the same map as their suffering."[12]

On the same map, on the same globe: lines overlap and intertwine.

1777: Eight hundred and sixty-one Black soldiers from Saint-Domingue join US rebellion forces in their fight against the British in Savannah, Georgia. Thirty-four die.[13]

1779: The son of a Haitian woman and a French pirate establishes a trading post along Lake Michigan. Today we call it Chicago.[14]

1794: Louis Duclos starts the first newspaper in New Orleans. He is a Haitian refugee.[15]

1803: After Haiti finally throws them out, the French reevaluate the viability of their foothold in the Americas. A few months later, France sells the Louisiana Purchase to the United States.[16]

Aristide's changes had economic ripples. His ambition was for the poor "to move from destitute misery"[17] to "poverty with dignity."[18]

1862: The US recognizes Haiti's autonomy, fifty-eight years after Haiti's independence.[19]

1868: President Andrew Johnson suggests that the United States annex Haiti and the Dominican Republic to secure the Caribbean for itself.[20]

1888: "Haiti is a public nuisance at our door," says US assistant secretary of state Alvey Adee.[21]

1893: Frederick Douglass delivers a speech at the Haitian Pavilion at the World's Fair in Chicago.[22]

My subject is Haiti, the Black Republic; the only self-made Black Republic in the world. I am to speak to you of her character, her history, her importance and her struggle from slavery to freedom and to statehood. I am to speak to you of her progress in the line of civilization; of her relation with the United States; of her past and present; of her probable destiny; and of the bearing of her example as a free and independent Republic, upon what may be the destiny of the African race in our own country and elsewhere.

In Greek or Roman history nobler daring cannot be found. It will ever be a matter of wonder and astonishment to thoughtful men, that a people in abject slavery, subject to the lash, and kept in ignorance of letters, as these slaves were, should have known enough, or have had left in them enough manhood, to combine, to organize, and to select for themselves trusted leaders and with loyal hearts to follow them into the jaws of death to obtain liberty.[23]

From both within and outside Haiti came support for the military that Aristide was trying so hard to scale down. "So long as the US supported it," writes Peter Hallward, "the army was too powerful to dislodge; without an armed wing of its own, the popular movement could not confront [the army] directly."[24]

"Our privileges," Sontag continues, "may—in ways we might prefer not to imagine—be linked to their

suffering, as the wealth of some may imply the destitu-
tion of others."[25]

Rich *because* some are poor: this is a sentiment that
defies American exceptionalism, yet reverberates in
the American ethos. Rich because slave labor is free.
Successful because this land was stolen. An easier life
because my skin is lighter. So what does this say of the *I*,
the industrious one who nevertheless worked hard? This
is an uncomfortable question for the national psyche.

"The poor person does not exist as an inescapable fact
of destiny," Gutiérrez writes. "His or her existence is not
politically neutral, and it is not ethically innocent. The
poor are a by-product of the system in which we live and
for which we are responsible. They are marginalized
by our social and cultural world. . . . Hence the poverty
of the poor is not a call to generous relief action, but a
demand that we go and build a different social order."[26]

It became clear that Aristide's new government, with
its increased wages, tariffs, and taxes and its increasingly
clean house would change the way trade worked for the
Haitian elite and US business interests. A coalition of US
businesses requested that Aristide replace some of his
ministers of state with their own handpicked candidates.
The president declined.[27]

*1914: President Woodrow Wilson seizes control of the
Haitian National Bank using US marines. For "safekeeping,"
he takes $500,000.*[28]

1915: Under Wilson, the United States invades Haiti to

"protect US assets" and prevent German influence. Haiti happens to have strategically located ports and a wealth of natural resources and manpower.[29]

1934: Nineteen years later, the United States withdraws from Haiti.[30]

On the night of September 30, 1991, there was nothing the small presidential security league could do when the Haitian army—with "unofficial but unequivocal US support," as Hallward writes—captured Jean-Bertrand Aristide and put him on a plane to Venezuela.[31]

The first fairly elected ruler in Haiti's history had been in office for less than a year.

After the overthrow, some countries refused to recognize the new Haitian military government. One of them was Cuba.

"So I studied medicine in the Dominican Republic," says Gardy.

Gardy lived in Santo Domingo for almost a decade. Many of his classmates were wealthy Dominicans and Haitians who assumed he too was a member of the elite class who could afford medical school. Gardy decided early on that it was easier not to correct them.

Highway 2 after Miragoâne is full of little towns. As we come upon one, Gardy asks me if I've ever tried *douce macoss*.

I haven't. What is it?

"You'll see."

*

Sometimes his classmates wondered why Gardy didn't have a nice car. He only ever invited one or two of them over to his apartment. It wasn't impossible to pass as "one of them," he says, especially since he did well in school. "They thought, since I came from high class, my money talked for me. My money gave me value." Gardy says. "They're treating other Haitians working construction in the Dominican Republic like they're nothing. It's very sad. People really evaluate you for what you have."

When Gardy sees the stand for *douce macoss*, he pulls over. He says he'll be right back, walks up to the powder-pink metal siding, and orders. The yellow, green, and blue letters of the sign hide rust. He leans against the chest-high counter lightly, arms bent, dress shirt half-untucked from sitting in the car. The round face of his watch glints. A woman works behind the counter and a young girl, barely tall enough to see over the ledge, looks at me. We wait.

Gardy graduated from medical school at the top of his class. His standing earned him a job in the Dominican Republic.

He returns to the car with a brown bag.

"You have to try one while you're here," he says. "I've tried them all over, and these are the best *douce macoss* in all of Haiti."

Unwrapped, the brick Gardy hands me is a cookie,

49

two inches tall, with half-baked dough and chunks of chocolate.

Coming back to Haiti after graduating medical school wasn't a given for Gardy.

I bite and a rush of sugar envelops my tongue. It's the most sugar I have ever tasted; it dances between sticky-sweet and rich-sweet. The warm dough and chocolate melt with caramel and condensed milk.

"Mmmm."

The more I chew, the sweeter it becomes. It's almost too much.

On the next bite I close my eyes.

When someone is sensitive, sometimes we say they're *sweet*. It's a compliment of sorts, commending their kindness but with the understanding that you can overdo it. Too sensitive and you flirt with sentimentality.

Gardy teases, "Now don't eat it all or you'll be sick."

This cookie brick grows with every bite.

I wrap it back up and put it in my bag, thanking him, telling him I'll save it for later.

"It was a hard decision, to come back to Haiti," he says. "As the oldest child, you have a lot of responsibilities. But when you live in another country, there is some distance from that."

*

I would forget about the *douce* and days later find it still in the front pocket of the backpack, covered in ants attracted to the sweetness.

Distance protects. Too much sensitivity and you fall apart, pieces carried off crumb by crumb. But it also obscures, separates. Offers a chance to forget.

Eventually, though, Gardy returned.

"I decided to come back to Haiti because I felt it was the right thing to do."

Six

T/here.

In *The End of History*, Francis Fukuyama uses Hegel's dialectic to think about the process of arriving at the last form of government.[1] The dialectic goes like this:

Thesis + Antithesis = Synthesis
Thesis + Antithesis = Synthesis
Etc.[2]

The synthesis emerges from commonalities in a thesis and its antithesis.

My professor used to write this on the board, and when he did, he would circle the word *thesis* from where it sat inside *synthesis* and start the process over, writing *antithesis* above it.

If the book that got me to Haiti is both a vehicle and a destination, then the process, at any point, is a place. It's a stepping stone and its own complete thing, a process and a whole. A kind of becoming.

I want to know what happens in history's slash—what goes on in the circling, and how attention makes something a transition or a destination or both.

What is in the remnants? What evolution or distancing occurs in the act of circling and pulling something out? The circle is a focusing lens that, by its definition, excludes.

Thesis. Antithesis. Synthesis.

When Gardy moved back to Haiti from the Dominican Republic in the late 1990s, he quickly found a job with a US-based nonprofit that works toward fairer labor standards by examining international supply chains.

"They paid me ten thousand US dollars a month!" he says. "And this work is in Haiti. At a nonprofit—a nonprofit!"

One hand holds the steering wheel and the other waves around.

"Can you believe it?"

This was a wild sum, he said, not even to use his medical degree but to inspect factories. His job was to determine if working conditions were safe enough.

"These were big companies that contracted with factories," he says. "Like Gildan, Reebok, and others."

Factories that were safe enough. *Enough* suggests the required, the bare minimum. But it is never fixed, nowhere near standardized. It depends on your point on the map.

*

"There's a standard here, and there's a standard there," Kirsty had said to me back at the birthing home. She, a Canadian expat, had flipped her *here* with her *there* as she became more fixed in Haiti. We're sitting in the office she shares with the clinic's driver as she covers for a nurse who is sick today, signing patients' paperwork and scheduling their next appointments.

"A good example of that is MSF, Doctors Without Borders," she says. The organization (*Médecins Sans Frontières*) started off as a French coalition of doctors who responded to wars and disasters in the early 1970s.

"MSF says they do development, but that's because really—and Haiti is a good example—they come in as a relief organization and they don't go away for a long time."

The organization has been in Haiti since 1991, Cambodia since 1979, Sudan since 1979. And the list goes on.[3]

"Their idea is to get an amazing hospital that's like a machine," Kirsty says. She meets my eyes and leans in.

"They want a hospital that works really, *really* well and provides amazing care for free. That's phenomenal, but they pay their staff exorbitantly in comparison to the pay scale that already exists in the country. When you have organizations that come in and pay their employees a lot more money, you inadvertently—or not—set the bar high.

"The expectations of employees change," she says. "And in a way, they should. But in another way, it's terrible because it sets up a competition that compromises what the state can afford and it compromises all of us other organizations that sit closer to public health principles."

The controversy of *enough*. How do you set the standard?

Article II of the Nongovernmental Organization Code of Conduct for Health Systems Strengthening, a treatise published in 2008, declares: "NGOs will enact employee compensation practices that strengthen the public sector," because signees "recognize their collective history in creating inequitable pay structures."[4]

It's a document that admits wrongdoing and blurs *here* with *there*. Rich *because* they are poor. It is not enough, the treatise says, to bring the health standard of the *here* of the NGO's home country to a place or a handful of places over *there* in the "aid" country. Rather, the *there* must be built across the board, connecting places through public health infrastructure, to redefine what is *enough*. It will be slower but, the code argues, it will stick.

"The biggest infrastructure in this developing country," Kirsty says of Haiti, "is the state. There's a public health system that exists. It's not great, but it's not by any means weak. It's been there for a long time. They have a salary scale."

"It's there," she says again. "It exists."

Gardy's approval of Haitian factories was crucial to their securing contracts with big manufacturers.

"These companies offer million-dollar contracts, so the deals are very important to the factory owners," he explains. They can make or break a business.

The traffic on Highway 2 is picking up, the closer we get to Port-au-Prince.

Once, when Gardy was visiting a factory that produced underwear, T-shirts, and jeans, an executive at the factory asked to meet. Gardy agreed.

I picture Gardy walking into the man's office, both of them in suits, and the man getting up from behind his desk to shake hands. They sit in cushioned club chairs on the near side of the desk, maybe, and the man asks Gardy if he'd like a drink and what he thinks about the tour. He asks how Gardy's family is doing. Gardy says fine. The man leans back and rests his elbows on the chair's armrests.

It plays like a Hollywood movie reel in my mind, in part because I don't know what to imagine and in part because, in the cinema, a scene can feel like it is unfolding *just* for you and simultaneously be entirely separate from you.

"He offered me a bribe," Gardy says.

The man would pay $40,000 for a passed inspection.

"I looked at him as he said it. I had to keep my face neutral. I told him I'd think about it."

To pass a car on this two-lane coastal highway, wait for a relatively flat and almost straight stretch; it will take a while to find one. Then shift and hit the gas. Use the middle lane that has somehow appeared in front of you because the cars coming at you are hanging onto the road's perimeter. Squeeze through and merge.

"If I took the bribe, I would be just like all the politicians who were part of the corruption," Gardy says. "If I said no, they would go after my family. My family would be in danger."

"So, I thought about it. I thought about it for a week. What could I do?"

"I went to the nonprofit and told them I quit."

The organization flew Gardy to their headquarters in Boston to persuade him to stay.

"They said, 'Do you need more money? We can't give you more money.' I said, 'I don't need more money. I don't want more money. I just quit.' The next day, they offered me more money. I didn't take it. They kept me there for a week, trying to convince me. I never told them why I quit."

Gardy's fingers play over the steering wheel with fast taps as we shift the conversation to other nonprofits.

"I heard of an NGO the other day that gave out two hundred US dollars to all of the families living in the program area," he said.

"It was supposed to last them six months. The total cost of the program was a hundred seventy-five thousand dollars! Think of what else you could do with that money. Think of it! You could build something."

"Pay salaries, buy medicine, get new healthcare equipment," I say.

"Yes, exactly."

"So why would they do that?"

"Why *would* they do that?" he says. "Why would they?" Gardy is speaking from the bottom of his lungs and the back of his throat. "Because if they do something sustainable, that *really* helps people not be poor, where would the group be? What would they do?"

He waits for me to answer.

"They'd be out of a job," I say. "Or out of volunteer work."

"Exactly."

Dependence is a word that gets thrown around often in the conversation about aid—whether it's foreign or domestic.

Dependence, as in a program *breeds a culture of dependence.*

Breeds, as in animals, the nonhuman kind.

But one term that's hardly mentioned: *symbiosis.* As in the suckerfish who attaches to a whale and eats its scraps while keeping it clean.

There is a dependence on the savior, but also a dependence *of* the savior.

Without people to save, what is the savior?

How do I orient myself, if not in relation to you?

Gardy is talking about changing roles. He is talking about the endgame. He wants to know, he says, how aid groups can work themselves out of a job.

"Let me tell you another one," Gardy says. "A program gave out bags of rice. One for each child in the family as part of a two-year program. What do you think happened?"

It didn't take long, he says, for people to start borrowing children and alternating days at the distribution point. Then rice farmers in the area stopped growing because their market had dried up.

"Then—remember this is a two-year program—people started having more children," Gardy says. "And what happens after two years? The group leaves and the community is worse than when they began."

Gardy tells me about another program. "They decided to give participants who were [HIV] positive free medicine, a new house, food, a little money to start a business, and paid for their children to go to school."

"Okay," I say. This seems to address the root of many diseases: poverty.

"They give them a house and medication and food and money *and* school!" Gardy says. "Well, many people came back a week after they got the money and said: 'I was at the market and someone stole my money. Can I have more to start my business?'"

"Did they give out more money?"

Gardy shrugged.

"Do you think the people were lying?"

"I think it's a lot to give. More people got tested. They heard about what happens if they're positive."

"If they're HIV negative, they don't get anything?"

"Yes. And their neighbor has a new house and money to start a business. Imagine."

"Mmm."

"Imagine." His voice cracks to a whisper. "*Imagine* people being *sad* that they're negative."

I blink.

"Mmmhmm," Gardy says to the empty air.

"People are *upset* because they *don't* have HIV?"

"Yes, because they're given so much."

No words come. People wanting HIV for the benefits.

"It's too much," he says about the program.

"It's too much," I repeat. Too much to grasp, to take in.

Every now and then as we drive, blue glances of the sea shine through the Land Cruiser's windows.

After Gardy's factory inspector job ended, he worked in the health care field, but tended to disagree with the vision of the groups he worked for.

"Dr. Smith had said to me, 'I used all my savings to send you to med school. I have one request of you: when you are done, return to your country and do good work.'"

Was it fair for Dr. Smith to ask Gardy devote his life to Haiti?

In 2008, Gardy began OSAPO: Organizasyon Sante Popilè, or Public Health Organization. He started with a group of his friends who were doctors and nurses. They decided to set up in Rousseau, that tiny mountain town north of the capital where Gardy had played soccer and met Dr. Chalestin years before.

The next stretch of Highway 2 will take us through Léogâne.

At OSAPO, Gardy decided to charge a small fee for the clinic visits. Thirteen Haitian dollars, or about five US dollars, includes the doctor visit and basic medicine and tests. The cost for additional tests is posted on the wall at the back of the waiting room, near the pharmacy window.

I ask if that's reasonable in Haiti, where 80 percent of the population lives on less than two US dollars a day.

"Most people can pay," he says.

"What if they can't?"

"Most people can."

Léogâne is about twenty-six miles from Port-au-Prince.

The patient fee doesn't even dent the actual cost of the patient visit. OSAPO relies heavily on outside grants and donations. In addition to the clinic, OSAPO funds community health workers like Louna, who walk miles to see patients at their homes. They also run a nutrition program with a learning garden and vegetable seeds, a chicken and coop program, and a sanitation team that builds toilets.

*

Léogâne, three years, six months, and ten days before Gardy and I pass through it, had a population of a hundred thousand people.

Later I will hear from the staff at OSAPO that the clinic has never turned a patient away because they could not pay. Gardy would never advertise, "If you can't afford it, we'll pay for it." He says the fee is required. And yet. This *Can you afford it?* conversation is for insiders. It can happen if we share a *here*.

"But if we give everything out for free," Gardy says, "what are we teaching?"

Léogâne, three years, six months, and nine days before Gardy and I pass through it, was the epicenter of the 2010 earthquake.

Seven

.

January 12, 2010.

Haiti was struck by an earthquake.

Its magnitude: 7.0 on the Richter scale, which is to say a lot, which is to say devastation, hell, wreckage, torment, pure destruction, which is to say the city shook its bones clean from its flesh.

Two hundred thirty thousand is the number recorded for deaths, but there were likely more.[1] More than 300,000 were injured,[2] many of whom lost limbs, in a place where one's body is intimately tied to one's work, one's survival.

It came at 4:53 in the afternoon.

[CLICK]
/image:
/image:
I do not know how to describe the photos now, years later.

Tremors—the land swelling and falling in waves, like how a sheet ripples when you snap it above a mattress— came for days afterwards.

With each ripple, people thought it was happening all over again.

[CLICK]
/image:
Concrete ground back into sand, layered over everything, whitewashing—greywashing. Black bodies walking or standing against backgrounds of cement-grey powder.

Limbs protruding.

Haiti *was struck.*

We say it like this, in passive voice, to add space between the action (the strike, the hit) and the thing.
Was.
It happened; there is no agency.

[CLICK]
/image:
Half a decade after, I typed *Haiti* into Google Images. The second suggestion, still: *Haiti earthquake.*

[CLICK]
The subcategories of *Haiti earthquake,* in order:
/before and after
/destruction

/bodies
/map
/relief
/disaster children

[CLICK]
/image:
I looked at *map* as I prepared to click *bodies*.
I finally did.
Human beings, stacked like meat or coming up, half-covered, from the wreckage.
My stomach could not. These were daughters, nephews, grandfathers, aunts. These were people who went to work that morning, or who didn't, and were in their homes.

Haiti *was* struck.

It was inevitable, or at least blameless. An act of God or something beyond reach.
Inherent in the idea of accident is the removal of blame, of the possibility of prevention. But there is a reason Haiti's "poor" are *so* poor. And, subsequently, why the buildings are not made well.

"As objects of contemplation, images of the atrocious can answer to several different needs. To steel oneself against weakness. To make oneself more numb. To acknowledge the existence of the incorrigible," writes Susan Sontag.[3]

[CLICK]
/image:
The maps of the earthquake were so deliberate in their depictions. Blue water, green earth, and the area around Port-au-Prince like a rainbow bullseye, showing the severity of quaking.

"But there is shame as well as shock in looking at the close-up of a real horror," writes Sontag.[4] Maybe, she suggests, the only people looking should be those who could do something or learn something from it.

click click click click click
click click click click click click click
click click click click click

"The rest of us are voyeurs," she writes, "whether or not we mean to be."

The airport was destroyed. Flights either landed to the north in Cap-Haïtien or to the east in Santo Domingo. Medical supplies and water came in by helicopter.
News helicopter footage started making it back.
I sat, watching.
We organized and raised funds.
Still, it did not feel like it was enough. How could it have been?

There was *before* and then *after*. Years of cleanup, and there is still not much emphasis on *therefore*.

It was, as Paul Farmer writes, "acute on chronic," and therefore an "unnatural disaster." The earthquake was very bad; the existing conditions made it worse.

"The earthquake really broke my dreams," Gardy says. "In a lot of ways. The earthquake really broke my dreams."

He says it flatly, Highway 2 meeting us through the glass of the windshield.

The silence bends.

Nothing.

I decide to say something.

I don't want to ask why, because everyone knows why.

"Because of all the people who died?"

I can't avoid asking why.

"Yes," he says.

"My friend," he says, "my good friend was there. I had asked him to move to Port-au-Prince, so he could work for OSAPO. I recruited him. He was a physician."

His friend had not wanted to move to the capital—too hot, too crowded—but Gardy had convinced him. Nobody wants to live in Port-au-Prince, Gardy said, but this was a chance to build something and to implement their vision. It was the dream they'd always talked about.

They'd gone back and forth, but finally the friend moved with his family to the city. He and Gardy built the clinic together, driving back and forth to Rousseau.

"After the earthquake he called me," Gardy said.

Immediately following the quake, there was a window: some people had a few minutes of cell service before all went quiet.

"I was the person he chose to call. He was caught under the rubble."

"He said, 'I'm going to die in a few minutes, but I wanted to call you. I wanted to tell you not to feel guilty.'"

Gardy begins to cry, remembering. My eyes are wet too.

"He said, 'I'm glad I came here to work at OSAPO. I would not change anything. You must continue the work. You must go forward. Take care of my wife and child.'"

We are both crying.

"Sometimes, I do feel guilty." Gardy brings his hand to his face. "But I must move forward. I go forward with the work."

That day, OSAPO lost many physicians and nurses.

"The earthquake broke my dreams."

Eight

Before I left for Haiti, Sandra, the friend of a friend who introduced me to Gardy, said: "You know the saying about Rome? Well, in Haiti, it's all roads lead to Port-au-Prince."

I picture lines drawn around the globe, curving in and out from one another. Port-au-Prince is a mass of overlapping paths, like the center of a scribbled knot, full of starts, finishes, and the stuff of in between.

We were sitting on Sandra's couch, drinking orange juice at 6:00 p.m. and looking at pictures of Gardy's clinic on her iPad.

Re: Beginnings

From the sky above Haiti, you see the mountains rise to their sharp peaks. The ridges at this height are like wrinkles on sun-soaked skin.

Before the slaves, before the French, before Columbus, the inhabitants called their island *quisqueya*, cradle of life.[1] The Taíno lived there for 700 years.

"In their frenzied search for gold," says the *Visit Haiti* guide from 1956, "the Spaniards overran the island, unmercifully slaughtering or enslaving the defenseless natives, whose numbers were reduced from an estimated one million to some 200 in fifty years."[2]

During the plane's descent, buildings and then tents emerged. An enormous quilt of flapping squares was at once familiar and new; I recalled the photographs as I saw Haiti for the first time. Wheels down in Port-au-Prince.

Within two hours of landing, I was at the feet of Toussaint L'Ouverture (1743–1803), leader of the Haitian Revolution. Embronzed atop a pedestal, he stands straight in military attire, from cape to knee-high boots. His face is stern and his sword hangs down from his right hand.

In the early nineteenth century, shortly after L'Ouverture's death, the French naturalist Jean-Baptiste Lamarck published a theory about origins. It claimed a species could change in just one generation based on need and action.[3] If a giraffe stretches its neck again and again, its children will have a longer neck. Repeat.

It's a theory that lingers mainly because of Rudyard Kipling, author of *The Jungle Book*, "The White Man's Burden," and *Just So Stories*.[4] Lamarckism laid the groundwork, too, for Charles Darwin. How did the leopard get its spots? Why is the Ethiopian hunter's skin dark? It tries to answer why we are the way we are by connecting our bodies to a sense of *here*.

Across from L'Ouverture's statue stretches the iconic free slave: *Neg Mawon*.

He is "unknown" and muscular, crouched on one leg as the other extends behind. His torso stretches skyward and he holds a conch to his lips. He is enormous and sprawling in comparison to the upright L'Ouverture.

While the presidential palace across the street was fractured open in the earthquake—and still sits fissured when I see it three years later—*Neg Mawon* suffered not a crack.

We now dismiss much of Lamarckism for many reasons, one being that we know this much change doesn't happen in a single lifetime.

How many generations has it been since slavery in my home country's *here*?

Not even half a dozen.

We are not separate, Lamarck knew, from our circumstances.

L'Ouverture, once a slave, was freed in 1776. In August 1791, he helped the French quell the rebellions of white plantation owners who, in the wake of slave revolts, were demanding more autonomy from France and fewer rights for emancipated slaves. Some of the slaves who aided the French in fighting the owners' rebellion were then freed. L'Ouverture became the leader of this growing army of liberated slaves and slowly rose to control the colony.[5]

Four years after his rise, L'Ouverture wrote his staunch abolitionist views, and himself as governor for life, into the changing constitution.[6] It was drafted during the time of the French Revolution and Napoleon Bonaparte's rise to power.

Title II of the 1801 Saint-Domingue Constitution reads: "There cannot exist slaves on this territory, servitude is therein forever abolished. All men are born, live and die free and French."[7]

Women would not get the vote in Haiti until the Constitution of 1950, but L'Ouverture's phrase, "servitude is therein forever abolished," included women.[8]

Re: Middles

Port-au-Prince streets at dusk on a Sunday evening.

Cars flow from the highway into the side streets of the city. Neighborhoods refill with people who got away for the weekend.

Gardy and I are in one of these lanes, coming back to the metropolis of more than a million after a five-hour drive.

Port, as Gardy calls it, feels like a city on a hill. We drive through neighborhoods and he offers their names, while street games of soccer part in front of the Land Cruiser. To the left there's a mural. Below, a litter of empty plastic bags, formerly water sachets, sticks to the street. Tomorrow, we will head to his clinic in Rousseau.

Re: Beginnings

Lorelle D. Semley writes of the celebration of the 1801 Constitution of Saint-Domingue: "In an exuberant toast at the end of the day, L'Ouverture appealed to 'the external bonds of friendship and fraternity between the people of France and the people of Saint-Domingue.' But to issue such a constitution without consulting Napoleon Bonaparte's government in France directly challenged French colonial rule."[9]

General Charles Leclerc, Napoleon's brother-in-law, led an enormous force to the island. They claimed their mission was to fortify defenses from potential attackers. Their intention, however, soon became clear: overthrow L'Ouverture and reinstate slavery.[10]

L'Ouverture was captured, but when his troops learned of Leclerc's plan to restore slavery, Jean-Jacques Dessalines, one of L'Ouverture's lieutenants, took up the mantle of Haitian independence.[11]

A year of brutal conflict ensued. The land and the people were ravaged by war. Fields were scorched.

As the revolution approached its end, the death toll reached almost half a million—the vast majority of them non-Europeans.

As the French realized their weakening position, they sold the territory of Louisiana to the United States.[12] This purchase included the swath of land on which my ancestors would make their farm and their living, in the state I still call my home.

In January 1804 the country of Haiti celebrated its independence.

Re: Middles

The night Gardy and I arrive in Port-au-Prince after our first day of driving, I stay with another friend of Sandra's. Her husband is a music producer. She takes me around to see the homes they rent out before bringing me back to her own, where I will stay in a room that belongs to her preteen daughter, who is spending the summer in New York City with other family. My private bathroom has a toilet that's been painted gold and lacquered over. Set into the clear finish is US money—quarters. That night I pee into a pot of gold stamped with George Washington's face.

My host and I meet Gardy for lunch the next day at a restaurant near the US embassy. Along with another OSAPO doctor who is riding north to the clinic, we sit on the patio under a shade. The outdoor furniture arrangement feels lifted out of a catalog.

Gardy and the other doctor have been there for a while, so they wait. The buffet is expensive: lunch goes for about US $35. "We won't pay," my host tells me as we walk up to the food. "They," here she motions at the two male doctors, "will pay."

It is a foreign social understanding. It's as if everyone has agreed that any of us could pick up the whole tab, so it doesn't matter who does, and therefore the men will do it.

I don't remember what I ate—maybe cooked vegetables—but I do remember the same silver catering trays I'd seen back home, with candle burners under them. The food was a bit cold and mostly picked over and I felt, after a week at the birthing home, that my *here* was very far from the rural roads I'd walked with Louna just days before.

The American embassy nearby looked like it was made of concrete Lego blocks. It was the color of sandstone and imposing, sitting off a wide road with a dusty yard near some buildings that resembled strip malls. It seemed like an otherwise barren part of town.

Re: Beginnings

Liberté, égalité, fraternité: freedom, equality, brotherhood. These were the lofty tenets of the French Revolution, later reinterpreted by the American one. But it was Haiti where these ideals came closest to taking root.[13]

"Only in Haiti was the declaration of freedom universally consistent," writes Peter Hallward in his comparison of these three revolutions. "Only in Haiti was this declaration sustained *at all costs*, in direct opposition to the social order and economic logic of the day. Only in Haiti were the consequences of this declaration—the end of slavery, of colonialism, of racial inequality—upheld in terms that directly embraced the world as a whole."[14]

We don't always get to choose our *here*. But sometimes we can design its breadth: how far its boundaries reach across, over, and around our globes. We can decide what or whom this *here* includes.

Re: Endings, New Beginnings

"Only in Haiti."

If only victory could have held in Haiti. Had history paused, had the camera zoomed out on a battered but triumphant country, Haiti would be different today.

But instead, a different type of war brewed: one of continued oppression, institutional racism, and debtors' prison.

"The Haitian Constitution of 1804 was liberal," says the 1861 *Guide to Hayti*. "Its decrees have no longer any other than an historical interest. It recognizes the right of property in the country to belong exclusively to the men of African or Indian races, and has been maintained in every subsequent Constitution."[15]

In 1804, slave-owning countries, particularly the United States, dominated international trade. They viewed the Haitian revolution as a threat: what if slaves in the American South were inspired? What would become of the markets driven by their labor?

So when France, still reeling from the defeat, lobbied its allies to block Haitian trade, the United States and many other countries readily complied.[16] For the first time in more than a century, the resource-rich, export-heavy former colony became an island of isolation.

Haiti's economic legs were cut out from under it.

Breaking this boycott came at a steep price. In 1825, the entire French Atlantic fleet positioned itself just off Haiti's shore, ready to attack. Back on land, in "negotiations," the Haitian government agreed to compensate France for the loss of its slaves.[17]

The cost?

One hundred and fifty million francs.[18]

Beginnings, middles, ends: this is the stuff of stories we tell. We write our personal and political histories with order in mind, choosing what goes where. Meanwhile, the sections bleed into each other. And time makes everything into a past that informs the present.

Re: Endings, New Beginnings

One hundred and fifty million francs.

To repay the French for losses *they* suffered when slaves were freed.

One hundred and fifty million francs.

How much was it?

About as much as France's annual budget that year.

The US had paid less than half of that for the Louisiana purchase about twenty years earlier.

The sum was later reduced to 90 million francs.[19]

Adjusted for inflation and compound interest, 90 million francs is about US $21 billion.[20]

At the turn of the twentieth century, nearly a hundred years after the French fleet sat ominously offshore, 80 percent of Haiti's national debt was still being paid to France.[21]

"Haitians have thus had to pay their original oppressors three times over," writes Hallward. "Through the slaves' initial labor, through the compensation for the French loss of this labor, and then in interest on the payment of this compensation."[22]

In 1947, 143 years after its declaration of independence, Haiti paid the final installment to its colonizer.[23]

"Time and exuberance of both the land and its people

have healed the deep scars of slavery, devastation, and violence which darkened Haiti's history for so long," says Pan-America's bright-pink 1956 guide.[24]

During his second term in office in 2003, President Aristide asked France to repay Haiti and was promptly brushed off.[25]

After lunch I say goodbye to my host and get in the car with Gardy and the other OSAPO doctor. We will find Highway 1 and head north.

Nine

Human beings, we know, require water. It lubricates joints, cushions the brain and spinal cord, delivers oxygen, helps feed cells, regulates body temperature, and moves digestion forward.[1] There is nothing like it.

Water leaves our bodies through urine, sweat, and breath. It mostly enters through the mouth.

The part of the brain that senses thirst is the hypothalamus. This is also the part that maintains homeostasis, or that beautiful, delicate balance that counters external with internal. It responds to temperature and sleep, hunger and moods. It constantly checks the body's *here* against the world out *there*.

Gardy's clinic is about sixty miles from the capital, but we'll keep following the coast up the western side of Hispaniola and switch to backroads at the small town of Montrouis. We will pass through the Artibonite Valley. The whole thing will take us three hours.

*

The definition of *body of water* is broader than I first thought. I always knew the term referred to oceans, seas, and lakes, but it can also include ponds and swamps. Running water counts, too.

My *here* in the middle of Missouri appreciates these expansive qualifications. I am nowhere near a beach, but surrounded by bodies of water.

The human body is 60 percent water.[2]

For a while, the route Gardy and I take parallels the Artibonite River, which supplies much of Haiti's 150-square-mile central plateau with water. We're miles from this water; we can't see it, but I can feel its presence. Thirty-three months ago a cholera outbreak began on the central plateau in Mirebalais and followed the Artibonite watershed.

I will meet a patient at OSAPO who presents with bloody stools. He is sixty-nine and does not have cholera. He will lean over his lap, elbows on knees, as he speaks with a clinic doctor, draped in an oversized plaid shirt.

I will notice his puffy right eye and later learn this is a symptom of Chagas disease.

Chagas is endemic to Central and South America and the Caribbean.[3] It's something you catch because you're poor. Like malaria, it is transmitted by an insect bite, though not a mosquito. This bug thrives in walls made of mud or thatch or straw—the only kind most poor rural people here can afford.

This nocturnal insect, the triatomine bug, bites you, ingests your blood, and defecates on your skin. If you scratch around the bite and then rub your face or eye while sleeping, the Chagas parasite, *Trypanosoma cruzi,* can enter your body.[4]

Cholera, on the other hand, does not lie dormant here, waiting to flare up. It does not lurk in the walls and come out at night.

Until 2010, not a single case of cholera had been found in Haiti for over a hundred years.[5]

I ask Gardy if OSAPO has been treating a lot of cholera. They have. "There is a tent," he says.

"Still?" I say.

"Oh, yes. But it's nowhere near as bad as it was."

After the 2010 earthquake, the United Nations set up a base near the banks of the Artibonite and hired the cheapest company it could find, SANCO, to handle septic waste. Jonathon Katz, the Associated Press reporter who traced the cholera outbreak to Mirebalais, interviewed a man who lived next to the UN base. The man had watched the septic trucks dump raw waste into the pools of water by his house.

"When it rained, the pools overflowed," writes Katz. "Sometimes they ran downhill to the river. Sometimes they flowed the other way, toward Chery's house, and the smell would get so bad the family couldn't sleep."

Katz also found a broken PVC pipe leading from the back of the base straight into the Artibonite River.[6]

*

In *Illness as Metaphor*, Sontag writes: "Cholera is the kind of fatality that, in retrospect, has simplified a complex self, reducing it to sick environment."[7] Cholera only stops when treated as a crisis, an epidemic, a wave.

OSAPO's cholera tent has two rows of narrow beds lining each side, with an aisle down the middle, infirmary style. There is a UN seal stamped on the front. A UN-issued tent for a UN-issued disease.

I hear people talk about "flow" with longing. They want to make things flow or find their flow. What they mean is a smooth transition, like water pouring from a vessel, assuming the shape of its new home.

This attraction to ease of movement says something about our desire for less resistance. We are, it seems, on some basic level most at peace when there are fewer barriers between the self and the world surrounding it.

Where I'm from, to get clean water, I walk to the faucet. Unless of course it's not clean, which does happen in my *here* country. When it does, I am alarmed—my health is endangered, my trust betrayed.[8] My sense of standards, one of the things that defines my *here*, is shaken: if I do not have clean water, do I live in a *there*?

Back at the birthing home, when Louna taught people how to clean their water, it was "especially now":

post-cholera. Put the pills in it, she would say, and wait.

The man at OSAPO who walked "only" a few miles in his black rubber sandals for the Chagas diagnosis should be fine, the doctor says. The medicine will clear it up, at least until the next bug bites him.

With cholera, you can die within a handful of hours.[9]

Water is nearly 70 percent of the brain, 80 percent of the lungs, and 90 percent of blood plasma.[10]

I remember learning about water in the human body as a child: a *Magic School Bus* drawing of a body with water reaching past its midpoint, like a half-filled cup. I was a walking vessel. If I turned upside down, it would all rush to my head.

Some illnesses look pretty, even beautiful, under the microscope. Take Chagas, swimming like a snap pea in a pool of purple dye.[11] Cholera is not one of those illnesses. It's a collection of furry, stubby worms clumping together, demolishing the insides.

When *Vibrio cholerae* appeared in October 2010, Haiti was still sifting through earthquake wreckage from nine months before. The disease arrived first as a trickle, then as a stream, and then as a flood.

Cholera causes rapid loss of liquid. The body dumps itself out. Severe diarrhea and vomiting. Inability to hold down more fluid.

After the first case, it's a race: you need filters or water cleaning packets; stop eating raw vegetables if you don't know who washed them and with what. Be on constant alert.

The strain of *Vibrio cholerae* that ran into the Artibonite was eventually matched to an outbreak in Kathmandu.[12] As it turns out, the peacekeepers in Mirebalais were Nepalese. They'd had medical tests, per UN protocol, once—three months before departure. But this protocol did not call for a cholera test, despite the fact that they were coming from a *here* with an outbreak to a *there* with people who had not even a shred of immunity.

The cholera tests would have cost $2.54 per peacekeeper, plus an additional dollar per person for preventative medicine.[13]

Along Highway 1, the blues of sky and sea compete in brilliance. They come in glimpses through Gardy's window.

Seven months after the cholera outbreak, the UN finally issued a report.

It traced the outbreak back to its origin but excluded medical information from the soldiers, thereby denying responsibility. It claimed that a "confluence of circumstances . . . was not the fault of, or deliberate action of a group or individual," reports Katz.[14]

This, after not testing and treating the people crossing from *here* to *there*. This, after hiring the cheapest contractor to build the worst wastewater treatment. This, after denying involvement while simultaneously and surreptitiously testing the base that leaked the disease. But owning the mistake would have meant liability, which would have required money and action.

Confluence—that word we use when bodies of water collide. As if the contamination was inevitable.

The body can survive for more than three weeks without food. But it cannot go more than three to five days without water.

Since the outbreak in 2010—the fastest and largest spread of cholera in the world—more than 10,000 people have died and almost a million have fallen ill.[15]

In 2013, an advocacy group for Haitian rights filed a lawsuit against the United Nations for compensation on behalf of 5,000 cholera victims and demanded a public apology.[16]

In August of 2016—almost six years after the outbreak began—the UN admitted "involvement" in the epidemic.[17] This announcement was reported alongside the UN's independent investigator report, which said the organization's failure to take responsibility for the crisis was "morally unconscionable, legally indefensible and politically self-defeating." It also came with a promise to better address the epidemic.

Two months after that: Hurricane Matthew. Wind and water ripped across the island; with a waterborne disease, this is how you do the most harm quickly.

In December of the same year, the UN Secretary General, serving out the last month of his position, apologized for his organization's role. The focus of his apology was remorse for not doing enough about the outbreak sooner. He called for a new approach to eradicate cholera in a place where it had once been eradicated. The cost: US $400 million.[18]

As of early 2017, the UN had raised $2 million.[19]

Ten

We're turning from the sea now, Gardy and I, through a small town where the market crowd parts like a school of fish before the car and pours back into the street once it passes. We'll take rural mountain roads from here. When we drive by latrines and chicken coops with *OSAPO* painted on the side, we're getting closer.

"How did you rebuild after the earthquake?"

Really I am asking how you go on with a broken heart.

"It was slow," Gardy says. "We had to hire a lot of new people."

I ask Gardy how he finds his staff; he admits it isn't easy. They have to travel up to the remote clinic and stay there, hours from their family and friends. He's had to fire people who tried to take advantage of the clinic's resources. But for the most part, he says, the staff take good care of the clinic.

When we arrive at OSAPO and Gardy gets out, he glows. He smiles and waves at patients finishing up their visits. He asks about their families and their ailments. Staff tell him it's good to see him.

OSAPO is technically in Rousseau, but the single church, primary school, and one-room market that make up the town's center sit further toward the rushing river. The outside walls of the clinic are whitewashed stucco with bright-green letters spelling *OSAPO* and, under it, *Organizasyon Sante Popilè*. Like many Caribbean buildings, the clinic doesn't have heating or cooling: there are polished, built-in wooden shutters and blinds that open directly to outside air. Sunlight drips into the clinic, cast through the surrounding branches in the morning.

In this land with less than 1.5 percent of its original tree cover,[1] deforestation goes something like this: Poor peasants become poorer under trade policies. When the United States subsidizes its own domestic rice, for instance, and forces Haiti to ease tariffs on imported rice, it undercuts the local market.[2] Haitian rice can't sell when the US bounty flowing into their country is cheap or free. Farmers in Haiti can no longer make a living off their grain, but they still need fires for cooking. Trees are cheaper than coal, so trees go first. The land erodes more quickly. Stripped land makes it harder to farm, income keeps plummeting, and now people need cheap fire more than ever.

Satellite photos of Hispaniola island show the Dominican Republic as lush and Haiti as barren.[3] Yet, in places, you can walk through a Haiti lit green by foliage. Rousseau is like that. I think of Mackenzie, whose family owns a swath of land he is turning into a farm. He and Kirsty, in their time away from work, are involved with reforestation efforts.

By high noon the sun bounces off OSAPO's bright white tile floor, enough to make you squint. Come evening, patients have mostly returned to their homes, and the light echoes back out into the forest.

The tiles extending from the waiting room to the front porch will someday meet those of the new nutrition and maternity wings that are currently being built. A woman mops them over and over each day, keeping the first steps into the clinic pristine.

When I arrive, there are other *blans* visiting OSAPO—medical students from Michigan—and we check out the price list one day after the clinic closes. It's on the back wall of the waiting room. We marvel at its straightforwardness. The expenses are in Haitian dollars; most services and medicines do not exceed a few US dollars. Having a healthcare menu with services and costs listed is utterly foreign to us. Beyond the waiting room is a central area, with an open ceiling revealing the second-floor staff residence. Like spokes of a wheel, the corridors of OSAPO's main floor spin off from this open-air center. To the right, patient consult rooms; walk straight back and find a hospital area sectioned off with half-walls and beds; on the left is the delivery room; the back left corner holds the operating theater.

The surgeon comes on Wednesdays.

The staff residence upstairs has a big kitchen, an office for the accountant, a conference room, two bathrooms, and three bedrooms. The bunks are made up of old hospital beds. There's one room for women, one room for men, and a small room for whomever. A balcony extends from the central hallway. From it you can hear the rushing river and see the green mountainsides.

On a main wall upstairs, in large typeface, a mural reads: *BE THE CHANGE YOU WISH TO SEE IN THE WORLD.*

Sandra had pointed it out in photos before I left home.

Gardy asks me about it shortly after I arrive. I think of where I last saw those words: on an enormous matte-black coffee mug. A going-away present from my old boss, with the message: "I saw this and thought of you."

OSAPO is a *there* full of committed, courageous people. Some mornings in my *here*, I think: *All I have is this coffee mug.*

"I saw the mural," I say. "I like it."

Gardy hangs around OSAPO for an hour or so, visiting. This is where we'll part, at least for a while. He will continue north to a meeting in the port city of Cap-Haïtien. I'll stay at the clinic for about a week and, when he's here again, catch a ride back to Port-au-Prince.

Most OSAPO staff cycle their days at the clinic—usually three or four—with time in Port-au-Prince, where many live. In the evenings, several of the women on staff bring a laptop out on the balcony to play a Tae Bo video. It's the same recording as the VHS tapes I remember my aunt had packed into her living room. The teacher hollers English from fuzzy speakers: "Roundhouse kick! Jab!"

These exercise sessions start around 8:00 p.m., when darkness nears and the air begins to cool. The staff line up and sweat. Sometimes they put on music and dance afterward.

One evening the other *blans* and I walk down the gravel road from the clinic. We veer off onto a footpath up one of the mountains—a not-quite-trail that men, women, and kids are scaling in flip-flops. I climb in my hiking boots up the steep slopes of dry, fine gravel with sweat on my palms, feeling too close to a tumble.

A roar erupts. There, on the plateau past the road and beyond the river, is a field with a soccer game in full force, the downing rays illuminating the pitch like stadium lights. From up here, we can see the standing crowd lining the perimeter of the field, cheering for the goal someone has scored.

Bodies wearing two colors dart back and forth. The field breathes—thumps. Players zip over the grass and hundreds of people on the sideline pivot, following the ball. You can feel the hum of the field, even from here.

The Saturday after the game, the *blans* and I return to the plateau to play catch. It seems more ordinary in the morning, void of crowds and far from dusk. An aide from the clinic has shown us—after witnessing our attempts to toss and chase a Frisbee on the river's rocky shore—how to get up to the field. We meet a few children along the way and walk together.

To get to the field, take the main road as it slopes downhill until you hit the rock marked by graffiti. Turn right, wind down the sharp bank, and when you reach the river, take your shoes off. The young girl in the blue-and-white plaid blouse who has followed the *blans* will now want to be the guide, and she will straddle the river rock, ushering the *blans* through the current. Her denim skirt will not get wet because she knows how to do this, but you will step gingerly in the cold current that runs with purpose. After crossing, catch some dirt and pebbles in your socks as you walk up the bank and through the forest; pass the house with the goat tied up outside. Climb until you hit the plateau.

As we toss the disc, more kids stream out of the houses to join us; it's not a school day. There are nearly thirty now, and the catch competition is fierce. One girl runs hard after every throw and, when the Frisbee hits the ground, plants her feet and swings to box out her competition as she scoops it up. Her main competitor is a boy who tries to chase down every pass. I am terrible at Frisbee. When I toss, I miss my mark by a mile.

As I migrate to the sidelines, a young woman with a big round basket of laundry on her head crosses the field. She's heading to the river and makes eye contact as she walks by.

"*Bonjou*," I say.

"*Bonjou*."

She stops close to me and smiles. She's tall—an inch or two taller than me—but easily twenty pounds lighter.

"Give me money," she says.

I wrinkle the elevens between my eyes.

"I don't have any money," I say. "See?" I stick my hands in my pockets to show they are indeed vacant.

"Give me this," she says, examining my digital watch, gently holding my wrist at eye level.

"No," I say. It's a hand-me-down, nothing special, but I use it every day.

She frowns. "Give me this," she says again, looking at the numbers.

I say no.

She releases my hand, keeps walking.

It's not the first time I've heard it: *Give me money*. In fact I nearly gave her the watch. Another common call, usually from kids in the street: *Blan, give me one dollar*. This is the ask: you're *here*, you've flown to Haiti, you've made it all the way to the middle of this field—surely you can spare it. This is because I am a *blan*, yes, though *blan* is not just about whiteness; it is about foreignness. A person from "Japan, India, or even Cameroon," writes Katz, is "most likely a *blan*."[4] Being *blan* means having access. It means the ability to choose to come *here*. It means you have means.

After she drops my hand, I feel a tightening in my stomach. My face is hot. I am uncomfortable with the confrontation and unsure I've made the right decision, or that there is a "right decision."

I should have expected this collision. In some ways I came *here* for it. And yet my body tells me I must have also thought I could avoid it. That I could hold myself separate.

I keep walking across the field. I can still feel her touch on my wrist.

Eleven

Waking up at OSAPO, I hear birds chirping, the river rushing, and, if I lay around in bed long enough, one Haitian pop song that someone plays on repeat as they get ready.

On Wednesdays, an outside nutrition program visits. It's run by a woman in her mid-twenties named Rebecca. She is from Texas, and when she says *y'all* with a light lilt I can hear her home. She wears a moisture-wicking T-shirt and loose cargo pants. Rebecca used to be a nurse in the children's intensive-care unit on the graveyard shift.

Rebecca and the two Haitian nurses on her team work for a nonprofit that provides ready-to-use therapeutic foods, or RUTFs: high-calorie premade food used clinically to treat malnutrition. This team works out of clinics, churches, and schools in a large coverage area. Mothers enroll their malnourished children and return every six to ten weeks for packets of a special kind of peanut butter called *medika mamba*. It's full of 500 of the "right kind of calories." In theory, these children go from being at risk to being stable.

When you go to Haiti, you bring something with you. Supplies, equipment, assumptions. I used to think I wouldn't pack stuff, because if everyone did, wouldn't that hurt the market? It does, and everyone does. You don't squander the opportunity for a guaranteed delivery. My hosts asked me weeks ahead of time to bring certain things, and I listened.

Packing for Haiti is a game of skill. To play well requires providing what is requested, but only within the confines of the suitcase. You want the weight—tangible weight— as close to fifty pounds as you can get it. No going over.

Dozens of mothers awake at dawn to walk to OSAPO for the nutrition program. They do this every week until their child "graduates." Of the fifty or sixty children, just one is accompanied by a father. His wife is sick, it turns out. As they wait, he has to ask for help from another mother to change his youngest's diaper. They convene on some benches near the low walls of the clinic's open back room. The line behind them extends out the door and around the corner, nearly reaching the cholera tent.

In the days before Rebecca's visit, the *blans* and I shadowed Dr. Mario. On his third pregnant patient of the morning, he handed me the tape measure after she laid down. The other *blans* had already measured.

"Oh wait," he said. "You're not in medical school."

"No," I said, accepting the tape measure.

"But, oh well," he said.

He stood at my side while the woman reclined. He had introduced us at the beginning of her visit. I asked if she minded.

"No, go ahead," Dr. Mario said.

When I asked Dr. Mario what the patients thought of our presence, he said, "If it was Port-au-Prince, they would not be okay. Here, we are in a close community. They're okay with you."

What does it mean, the *laying on of hands*?

Practitioners of herbal remedies and medicine men did it. Ancients sought oracles, looking for elixirs or wisdom or touch. Isaac blessed Jacob and followers reached for Jesus's robe. The line between spirit and medicine is a blurry one.

To touch is holy.

See a child who suffers severe malnourishment go from the hard, protruding belly and rust-colored hair of kwashiorkor to a soft, full stomach. See his arms fill out from enough protein. See his face become his own again.

Really, you can see it. Rebecca's team was given iPads to take photos and keep data on the patients.

"It *appears* to work well," she says, "but there are lots of problems."

Rebecca has to sync all of the iPads after the peanut

butter distribution finishes for the week on Wednesday, which requires consistent internet and power.

"Sometimes it takes me thirty-five minutes to load my email," she says.

The files, when everything is working, take twelve to sixteen hours to upload. She has to send them to a tech in the States, who syncs everything and creates a new version for her to download to each device. This has to happen in time for the next Monday of distribution.

"There have been two weeks when I haven't been able to download the information because we didn't have power and we didn't have internet. When I can't get that file back on all of the iPads, the three of us are scrambling to switch iPads, looking for a patient, and the moms get upset because they have to wait longer."

Uploading, syncing, and downloading usually takes thirty hours.

"It's worth it because when it works, it works great."

The picture thing is huge, I say.

"Yes. We're going to have a class on taking better photos," she says. "There's a lot of funds we could access, other than private donations, if we take photos well. Sometimes you can see the mom but not the child. I'm really working on trying to get the baby in the photo and nothing else."

Rebecca knows photos of children will elicit more donations. Is it sympathy the viewer feels *for* them—over *there*? Those innocent, "sweet" young things?

Compassion is defined as sympathy or pity *for*, but its

root, *compati,* is "suffer with."[1]

A photo of a malnourished child—just the child—in Haiti is a faraway *there* of someone who is also, because of their youth, in a different time. This gap in place and time creates space to feel *for.* This is not all bad—the donations it sparks might be essential—but it is worth noting that *feeling for* is not the same as *suffering with.* Then again, the photos might simply help you to see, to understand, what something faraway looks like.

Sometimes, upon seeing these photos, we say things like "I can't even imagine." What of this failure of imagination? Or perhaps this confession is more honest: a recognition that my *here* is so different it's nearly irreconcilable with *there.*

"We know how much we're giving each child every week based on the weight and age," Rebecca says. "And we know they're supposed to be eating only this, so if they're not gaining enough weight, we know something is going on."

"Do they not eat other food?"

"They can, but they're eating four or five 500-calorie packets a day, so it's already a lot just to eat what all's recommended."

How to measure the pregnant woman: touch the points of her hip, search for the bone. Here it is. Find it on the other side; stretch the thin tape marked with short lines across the round orb.

Tell the doctor the number. When he motions for the

measuring tape, hand it to him so he can confirm.

Before I left for Haiti, the stateside founder of the birthing home mailed me a package from Kansas City. I dragged the box in from the porch of my apartment and laid it down in my living room. I sliced through the packing tape, parted Styrofoam peanuts, and removed, among other things, umbilical cord clamps and rubber gloves. I hauled the supplies, packed in neutral-brown, busted-up luggage, across international borders and through checkpoints, where at least one generous person placed tape over the ripped suitcase like sutures, holding in the contents.

Kirsty, the Canadian birthing-home director, told me to check my North American goggles. They can make you see some practices, she said, like giving birth in the same room as another woman, as insensitive when it's normal here.

But it's also easy for *just different* to be a quick out. *Just different* acknowledges the role of culture, but it can ignore other reasons behind the difference.

That tape measure across the pregnant woman: I wasn't qualified. Dr. Mario's assumption of my competence was different, perhaps *just different* than the medical standards back home. The woman didn't seem to mind (*different* or *just different*?)—but I might not know if she did.

For OSAPO, Sandra had dropped off a packed duffel

and slipped me fifty dollars for the extra bag fee. No, I said. She insisted.

Sometimes the children in Rebecca's program don't gain. Mothers might split the peanut butter among their children or sell the packages.

Carrying weight is a careful balance of not too much and not too little.

I often think about intent. If you mess up, does meaning well lessen the blow? A maxim for children: *It's the thought that counts.* We say it to each other, too, for consolation. Sometimes we know it's not entirely true, but it's how we give each other a pass.

How far does the thought need to go for it to count?

Another maxim: *Think it through.*

The placebo effect is a phenomenon in medicine where intent is all that matters. It works because you believe it works. This belief, this faith, is what changes the outcome.

Rebecca says: "Since I've gotten here, I've had four moms try to sell the mamba." Of one woman, she adds, "When the Haitian nurses questioned her about it, she admitted it. She thought she could use the money she made to better support her family."

Gardy will tell me he is conflicted about the nutrition program. He likes Rebecca, but her program is temporary, until the nutrition wing is built and the gardening project lifts off. Rebecca wants to help with this next phase of OSAPO's development.

I measure another pregnant woman's growth later that day and give the numbers to Dr. Mario. He does not remeasure, only makes sure the numbers make sense in his chart.

Stretching the tape over the globe between the woman's hips, holding her hand to help her sit up, and bracing her as she stepped down off the table gives me a rush. I am *doing* something.

One afternoon I drag Sandra's duffel bag of supplies down to the clinic. No one in the residence upstairs knows what to do with it. It's late and nearly all the patients are gone for the day. A nurse I don't know is finishing paperwork and talking with a man. I approach her and motion, asking her to follow me to the bag in the empty room.

I unzip the bag and her eyes grow. We unpack forty-three pounds of baby onesies, creams, ointments, medicines, and bottle tops donated by Sandra and her church.

A volcano of charity erupts on the hospital bed.

In its wake, I feel the same rush.

I've hauled these almost-fifty pounds around for weeks.

"God bless you," the man says.

The woman echoes him.

Almost immediately, the warmth I feel becomes hot shame. How dare I be proud? I did not knit those hats; I did not buy those supplies. I am the messenger.

"No, no."

My feet move half a step back.

"It's not from me. Do you know Sandra? Sandra, the nurse who comes here sometimes?"

Nothing.

"It's her—it's from her church."

They say okay.

At the nutrition visit, one of the moms gives Rebecca a gift. The woman's eldest was too old for the program, but Rebecca knew from treating the younger daughter that the mother would give the child the allocated amount.

"So I decided to enroll her. The other nurses didn't agree, but it was my decision. And I think the mom knows that."

The mother waits to the side until Rebecca's station opens and brings her child up to be weighed. When Rebecca's done, she thanks her several times.

Then she carefully hands over an avocado and a bag of dried beans.

The avocado is as big as my hand. There's probably a cup of beans in the bag.

When Rebecca looks at the woman her jaw tightens, but she smiles.

"Thank you," she says.

Later, I ask if the woman grew that.

"I think so," Rebecca says. "The first week she brought food to us, we told her, 'Your daughter is very malnourished; you do not need to be giving us these things.' But it's her way of saying thank you. We've talked to the mom. We said, 'If you don't have any mamba, feed her this and she will gain weight solely from that.' I think she's getting to the point of knowing she can feed her daughter this, but because she's never done it in the past, it's a new process of education."

Other times, placebos are just placebos.
You just need the thing you need.

As it turns out, I was supposed to leave the duffel bag of supplies with the accountant. My host in Port-au-Prince, a friend of Sandra's, asked me about it after I left OSAPO. I told her the accountant had been gone all week; she'd caught a ride with Gardy up north to visit her family.

"Oh no, no, no," she said, and a rock began to grow in my stomach.

"I'm sorry."

"The accountant was supposed to count it all." She waved her hand as she spoke. My gaze drooped. "That's what I told you. Now we will not know how many of each item we have unless Sandra kept count when she packed the bag. Which I doubt she did."

"I'm sorry," I said again.

"It doesn't matter." She shrugged. "It's done."

I had written down all my host's instructions for OSAPO, from phone cards to beds, but there was nothing in my notes about the duffel. Maybe she'd told me; maybe she'd forgotten.

I knew by then the creeping understanding that it was so easy—inevitable?—to do harm while helping. Even if the help was asked for, even if the helping was a net good, and even though helping was a way of bridging distance.

Later I will ask Gardy about the woman with the avocado and beans.

"Even though many people have small gardens or plants in their yard, they don't know how much good eating their own food can do. They think they'll make more money selling it at market."

He'll tell me about a man who had his children work in the garden but not eat from it. He thought the money would help his family more.

"With our nutrition program, we're going to tell people they have to keep a certain amount of what they grow."

"The thing is," Rebecca says, "no matter what, I try to remember these moms are just trying to do what's best for their children."

Twelve

Three days before leaving Haiti, I sit with the three visiting *blan* medical students on the upstairs balcony of OSAPO. We watch the light leak from the horizon and talk about what we will miss. It comes down to people and place.

I'll miss the mountains and the verdant forests. The breezy, open windows and fluidity between indoors and out remind me I am in the highlands. I'll miss the people I've met who are committed to making their home better: the doctors, nurses, merchants, builders, farmers. Mothers and fathers. The spiced black rice, fried plantain, and fresh fruit juice.

We pack and unpack objects—they're the archive of the intangible. Objects root us in the physical world; they place us firmly *here* and separate us from *there*. But objects can also take us back, beyond borders of time and space. Every time I pick up my copy of *Mountains Beyond*

Mountains, I remember the first time I met Haiti through its pages. It was an experience, as I would learn after a decade of unpacking it, that shifted my understanding on some foundational level.

I went to Haiti because I wanted to see. I was there to ask, listen, and learn what the place could keep teaching me. I was there because I spent ten years not going. I was there, too, because I could be.

I am part of the roles I hold separate: the victim, the savior.

I am different from them, too.

It would take years before I recognized the rifts my influences had made, and years more before I understood how they rearranged the way I saw the world.

This self, fissured from those shifts so long ago, cracked from new experiences, is what I am learning. I am learning to hold it all.

As we sit on the balcony, Dr. Suzie comes out and leans over the rail, searching for a cell phone signal. She speaks quickly and hangs up. She starts to leave, then turns back to us.

"I have a patient who must go to Saint-Marc for an emergency." She points downstairs. "He has—"

She starts explaining in French, hoping the *blan* who spoke a few words of it will be able to follow. She can't.

Saint-Marc has the closest full hospital to the clinic.

Dr. Suzie hurries toward the hall. I get up.

"Is there something we can do to help?"

"I don't understand," she says.

"Can we assist?"

"Oh no. *Merci.*"

Dr. Suzie is at OSAPO for a year of residency. Unlike many of the other Haitian doctors in the clinic, she attended medical school in Haiti rather than the Dominican Republic or Cuba. Dr. Suzie speaks French and Creole, but she says she wants to practice her English. We bunk in the same room at the clinic.

"I think English is beautiful," she told me one evening.

"Why?

"I don't know. I just do."

She asked me to practice. That night we laid on our hospital beds in the dark and I slowly asked her questions about her family in English.

We think Dr. Suzie told us about the emergency downstairs in case we want to observe. One of us was shadowing her earlier today. We wonder if we'll be intruding. It is our habit to ask one another if we think we are in the way here, and I think mostly this is a good thing. Our *there* has become our *here*, yes, but it is not only ours.

Finally one of us says, "I'm going downstairs. She wouldn't have told us if she thought we'd get in the way."

One afternoon a few days earlier, I'd walked into our bunk to find Dr. Suzie shuffling pictures. She had the four-by-six photos in a white envelope and asked if I wanted to see. I sat next to her and she laid out her family. Her young daughters posed for a casual portrait. One wore pink. Another picture showed them playing with a pink ball. Her husband, also a doctor, was taking care of them while she was at OSAPO.

Three or four days here at the clinic, two or three there at home.

Many of Dr. Suzie's relatives live in Miami, Myrtle Beach, Tampa, and Boston. She and her husband will take their girls to visit her sister, a nurse in Boston, in January.

When she asked to see my family, I took out my phone and scrolled through. I'd forgotten how it felt to show pictures to a live audience. You explain who people are and smile down at the faces. Dr. Suzie cooed and complimented as I talked about each person.

As we put away our pictures, Dr. Suzie asked if I wanted to see her green card.

Yes.

It was at the bottom of her envelope and she extracted it slowly, set it on the white bed sheet, and ran her fingers over its paper cover, smoothing wrinkles that weren't there.

Part of her residence, she said, was here in Haiti because she didn't want to disappoint the doctor who had been her teacher. After she finished training, though, she and her husband wanted to move to the United States.

On their trip to Boston, Dr. Suzie and her husband planned to leave their daughters with her sister's family to begin school in the United States. They'd learn

English and get a better education, she told me. She and her husband would join them there when she finished residency.

Her eyes welled up as she said this. Mine did, too.

The man Dr. Suzie is treating downstairs has febrile seizures and convulsions.

In other words, he is overheating. One of the *blans* explains it to me like this, with increasing simplicity; it is a necessary translation.

This man is old, very old, straight and thin as plywood with grey and white dots of hair covering his face and head.

Press your forearms together: his thighs are thinner than that.

He wears red soccer shorts and a lightweight button-down.

The man can't stop sweating. His shirt is soaked through; a halo of moisture darkens his white hospital sheets as the nurses try to stabilize him. His temperature is 101.9 degrees Fahrenheit.

Add a degree for measuring by armpit and he's pushing a fever of 103.

When Dr. Suzie sees the thermometer screen, she grabs a calculator from a drawer and punches a few buttons to figure Celsius. One of the *blans* looks for the metric thermometer she saw earlier.

Ernante Cajuste, the young nurse who wears her navy clinic T-shirt tucked into low-rise jeans with a wide belt, prepares an IV. With the high ceilings and half-walls this late in the day, there's not enough light. Ernante squints at the needle.

A sound like water sloshing in a bathtub comes from across the room. The sole overnight patient sits up in her bed and vomits into a bucket. Her mother draws circles on her back. She is stable and recovering, plugged into fluids, waiting for morning to go home.

Ernante narrows her eyes, getting ready to stick.
"Mison!" she yells. "Mison!"
She uses the same voice for the young errand runner whether she's calling for phone cards or emergency medical supplies.
"Mison!" she hollers again.

Say it like this: Mi*son* as in *song*. Emphasize the second syllable and push from the diaphragm with confidence.

As Ernante calls, I ask the other *blans* if I should get my headlamp.
Mison arrives and she tells him to hurry up and bring the light. I waffle. He will get one.
Here he comes with a waist-high lamp from the delivery room.
He plugs it in at the man's bedside.
Click.
No light. He tries an outlet along another wall.
Click.
No light.

I hurry past the family who is gathering and back outside, where the neighbors are slowly filling the street. I take the stairs two at a time and run to my bag, pulling my headlamp from the small front pocket, and rush back down. One *blan* pulls me through the crowd and toward the man's bed. I press the button on my light.

My headlamp weighs maybe three or four ounces.
Five bulbs, three batteries, one button.
Press once for the bright middle stream. Press off.
Press once for the two side bulbs. Press and hold to dim.
I practiced these settings in my living room as I unpacked and repacked those boxes of supplies, quizzing myself. Press and hold one, two, three to trigger the red bulbs. Press off. I needed to know this light.

Wrapping the strap around my hand, I hold it high.
Light floods over Ernante's needle. She stops poking and makes a clean stick.

Later, Ernante and Dr. Suzie will say *thank you*.
Later, the *blans* will say, *We're so glad you had that.*

More of the man's family arrives. His daughter, wife, and friends are joined by young people trickling in and out, waiting in small clusters.
I count fifteen people near the bed.
His wife's arms are crossed and she shifts her weight back and forth.
Still, the man sweats. Still he seizes.

Maybe it's lessening. I don't know.

The sweat on his forehead, arms, chest, and legs does not bead. It downpours.

Ernante adds a catheter.

Two *blans* take the man's temperature again and show it to Dr. Suzie. With her permission, they cut his shirt down the middle, careful of his cords.

There is no ice, no temperature-controlled water, so the *blans* press their water bottles, slightly cooler than his body, into his heat centers: groin and armpits.

I don't understand why he hasn't been transferred to Saint-Marc.

Mison and the other *blan* bring a standing fan from the waiting room.

Again: *click* and nothing.

The closest live outlet they find is down the hall, so they stretch the cord taut and direct the air at him as best they can. It's barely a flutter.

I bring my other hand up, steady the light, switch arms, and keep the spotlight on the vibrating figure.

The man's thin wooden tongue compressor mirrors his frame. Please, please don't snap, don't splinter.

I touch the sweat on his shoulders, helping pull off the two halves of his shirt. I remember him feeling cool, but surely he wasn't.

Dr. Suzie prepares another injection. A hint of the bright wall trim shows through the syringe as she holds it overhead, giving the liquid a green hue. I will learn it is ceftriaxone, a broad-spectrum antibiotic. While it courses from the bag and pumps into the man, Dr. Suzie hustles around.

She finds some papers and writes.

She calls Dr. Felix, whom she spoke with on the balcony, again at his home.

Maybe she's hoping to stabilize the man before he travels. She prepares an envelope.

The crowd outside has been readying a stretcher. They are padding the gridded metal of a rust-red frame with cardboard, blankets, and pillows.

The man: he seizes. He stops. He seizes.

Nurses arrange him for transfer. They remove the catheter and hand the IV bag to a young man who will ride alongside him.

The old man's head must be kept over to the side when he gets to the truck so that, when he seizes, he won't choke on his own fluid.

Three men get closer and pick the old man up to carry him through the crowd and the halls, forgoing the wide stretcher outside.

He is naked, and before his carriers can navigate the angles of his body, he sinks and dips, legs riding a different wave than his rocking head.

They steady him along the plane of his torso and carry him.

The crowd parts.

I press my back to the wall, light held high, hoping the

doorframe is wide enough.

Outside, the tailgate of the old truck is welded shut. They will have to hoist the man up, minding the IV cord. A few people hop up into the truck bed to help with leverage.

Dr. Suzie shouts directions from the step at the passenger door. From this post, she can see over heads.

The men on the ground raise his torso, level him, move him over, and lay him down. His head nods to the side, too heavy for the neck.

Dr. Suzie presses the envelope into the wife's hand. I'm guessing it's medical notes and the hospital entry fee. I hear her say *Saint-Marc* and *OSAPO* as she gives final instructions.

As soon as the man is docked in the truck bed, the crowd recedes. They drive off.

One of Dr. Suzie's arms is crossed over her chest. The other hand is up by her face.

It's a thirty-minute drive to Saint-Marc.

I lower my lamp.

Dr. Suzie washes her hands in the chlorine bucket by the cholera tent and walks back inside.

At Saint-Marc, she says, the man will receive a cerebral scan, a sonogram, doses of sodium and potassium, and a ventilation tube.

He is eighty years old.

OSAPO needs an ambulance, she says.

It's around 9:30 p.m. We go upstairs to eat porridge

before bed. One *blan* brings out her miniature jar of Jif and we spread it across the white rolls, peanut butter sticking to our fingers and mouths as we talk with Dr. Suzie.

After we finish, Dr. Suzie gets on her phone. Later, she returns to our bunk to relax. A half-hour after that, she gets called back downstairs to the clinic. It's busy tonight. She doesn't come back until midnight.

The next morning, I ask what happened with the old man. Nobody knows.

I follow up with another doctor the day after. He's never heard of him.

To bear light: I admit it felt good to provide, to literally shed light where it was needed. But I wish my lamp had not been necessary. What was really missing was basic infrastructure: I don't know if the problem was the wiring in the walls or the power source.

To pack light: Before Haiti, I was a notoriously heavy packer. I would lug around maxed-out suitcases and test the limits of their wheels and zippers. I packed clothes and books I'd surely get to on *this* trip. These were items of adornment and totems of knowledge, and I figured the more I could haul around, the better prepared I would be. I was always a little embarrassed by their size, so I'd carry the weight up staircases and navigate doorways with quiet effort, rarely complaining and only occasionally second-guessing my choice.

That changed with Haiti. A carry-on backpack had

to fit what was mine for almost three weeks; checked bags were for supplies. I was nervous at first about what it meant to lay that weight down: would I have what I needed? What of the comfort my usual packed objects offered?

And so I asked: what did I *need* to make do? The list was short. And: what would happen if I didn't have what I needed? The answer was that I would be fine.

I left that last big duffel at OSAPO and zipped up my pack with my belongings. I was thinking of what takes up space, and what bears down on the shoulders but isn't held in a bag.

The things we want to carry; the things we want to hold; the things we want to leave behind.

Thirteen

.

When I catch a ride back to Port-au-Prince with Gardy and his physician colleague, Gardy teases me for nodding off in the back seat. The car is hot and rocks side to side over potholes. Even when we hit the highway, I have to fight to keep my eyes open. I have always found comfort in steady movement.

When I began to learn about Haiti over a decade ago, it was my introduction to injustice. There was a consistency: the poor were getting poorer from decisions made beyond them.

This pattern was like a pendulum: T-shirts *here*, excess *there*; surplus rice *here*, flooded markets *there*; and so on. To escape this rocking weight, all I had to do—I thought—was draw my line. Boycott certain brands, reject certain stories—close my eyes to them.

The two doctors and I stop at an orphanage on our

return to the city to drop off extra eggs from the chickens at OSAPO. We get out briefly, me still blinking my eyes open, and chat with the person working as one or two children help bring in the eggs. They come in big flats of several dozen, all shades of brown and speckled, dirty from the chickens and the earth. They remain unwashed, I learn, so they can sit unrefrigerated without rotting.

After my initial rage over a system of inequality, I sprang into action. It was not enough to live my life asleep; I poured my effort into fundraising, advocating, educating. Concerned with how much of a difference I was making and alight with the fire of fighting, I sought to make things right.

A ways outside the city, Gardy and I drive past neighborhoods being built with earthquake money. He criticizes the cheap building materials. They didn't hire much Haitian labor, either, he says.

"Look." He points to the open plateau around the pop-up housing. There's nothing but empty land surrounding the homes. "Where will these people go to work? How will they get there?"

What's the point, he's asking, of building it here?

Anyway, he says, construction has been halted; maybe they ran out of money.

Make things right. There was a delicious certainty that came with this clarity of conviction.

It came, too, with the desire to separate. I wanted to

erase my complicity and land firmly on the other side: the side of solution. I wanted to be *here*, while the causes of suffering were *there*. The ego in this.

As if I could be just one thing.

I will spend another day and a half with the host who has the toilet lined with quarters. She will take me that night to summer *carneval*, the Mardi-Gras-in-July parade, where she will work her connections for access to the biggest floats I've ever seen. Tractor-trailer cabs pull two-story structures, with stages for live bands above and tech command centers in the closed-off portions where the cargo would normally be. To gain access to these rigs, you have to have the proper colors of T-shirt and wristband from the sponsoring company. My host talks her acquaintances at the door into giving them to us.

By the end of the night, I carry three different T-shirts, all advertising Haiti's biggest cell phone company in a different color. When I return to the US, I give two away and use one for pajamas. It's not unlikely that these shirts will make it back to the island.

I went to Haiti *to keep learning how much I don't know.* What don't I know?

In a recent opinion piece for OSAPO, Gardy wrote that being Haitian, having grown up in that reality, "helps me understand our situation far better than those who have not been among Haitians long enough to *completely* understand the Haitian culture, its socioeconomic context, or the circumstances that impact the ways in which we live and die. I have seen numerous experts come to Haiti, especially after the earthquake, to 'solve' the problems of the Haitian people. They always believe they have the answer, and they reject Haitian opinions or decisions."[1]

Another way to ask: *What do I know?*

"NGOs need to improve the coherence of their projects. They need to understand they are here to work in partnership with the government and the population, not as an opponent. . . . They need to give the Haitian people leadership to decide what they want for themselves."[2]

I am still unpacking Haiti. I probably always will be.

I know that I still, as hard as it is to interpret, believe in justice—at least in the search for it. It might only come in small doses, but I believe there are ways to make and do some things right.

After Haiti, what objects do I hold onto?

My light. A few pieces of Haitian money. The books that sent me in this direction. The relationships, the people. These items are tucked away in drawers, placed on shelves, or carried with me.

These hands of mine unpack the objects piece by piece, seeing each one and feeling its weight.

Hold the memory here. Turn it over; look at it in this

light. What else do you notice?
  Time has passed. It had to, for clarity's sake.
  No—
  Time has passed because it had to.
  Now I look for clarity in its wake.

Notes

Chapter One

[1] Paul Farmer, "The Template of Colony," in *The Uses of Haiti*, 3rd ed. (Monroe, ME: Common Courage Press, 2006), 56.

[2] Edwidge Danticat, "How Jesus and Simón Bolívar Came to Share a House in Jacmel," in *After the Dance: A Walk through Carnival in Jacmel, Haiti* (New York: Crown Journeys, 2002), 39.

Chapter Two

[1] Mary Ruefle, "Poetry and the Moon," in *Madness, Rack, and Honey: Collected Lectures* (Seattle: Wave Books, 2012), 10–30.

[2] Tracy Kidder, *Mountains Beyond Mountains* (New York: Random House, 2009).

[3] Paul Clammer, Michael Grosberg, and Kevin Raub,

Lonely Planet Dominican Republic and Haiti (New York: Lonely Planet, 2011), 9–10.

4 Oxford English Dictionary Online, s.v. "guide," www. oed.com.

5 Ira Glass, "How I Got into College," *This American Life*, National Public Radio, September 6, 2013, www. thisamericanlife.org/radio-archives/episode/504/transcript.

6 James Buzard, "Tourist and Traveller in the Network of Nineteenth-Century Travel," in *The Beaten Track: European Tourism, Literature, and the Ways to Culture, 1800–1918* (New York: Oxford University Press, 1993), 47.

7 Pan-American Union, *Visit Haiti* (Washington, DC: Pan-American Union Travel Division, 1956), 2.

8 Kidder, *Mountains Beyond Mountains*, 10.

9 James Redpath, "The Vegetable Kingdom," in *A Guide to Hayti* (Ann Arbor: University of Michigan Historical Reprint, 1861), 44.

10 Oxford English Dictionary Online, s.v. "travel."

Chapter Three

1 Oxford English Dictionary Online, s.v."translate."

2 Ibid., s.v."interpret."

3 Clammer, Grosberg, and Raub, *Lonely Planet Dominican Republic and Haiti*, 264.

4 Pan-American Union, *Visit Haiti*, 29.

Chapter Four

1 Pietra Rivoli, *The Travels of a T-Shirt in the Global Economy: An Economist Examines the Markets, Power, and*

Politics of World Trade, 2nd ed. (Hoboken, NJ: John Wiley & Sons, 2015), 49–73.

2 Marc Silver, "If You Shouldn't Call It the Third World, What Should You Call It?" National Public Radio, January 04, 2015, www.npr.org.

3 Rivoli, *Travels of a T-Shirt*, 216–17.

4 Ibid., 229.

5 Trans-Americas Trading Company, www.tranclo.com.

6 Trans-Americas Trading Company, "Secondhand Clothing Export List," n.d., www.tranclo.com/buyers. asp.

7 Jonathan M. Katz, *The Big Truck That Went By: How the World Came to Save Haiti and Left Behind a Disaster* (New York: Palgrave Macmillan, 2013), 6.

8 Rivoli, *Travels of a T-Shirt*, 119.

9 Ibid.

10 Ibid., 149.

11 Ibid., 151.

12 Ibid., 150.

13 Oxford English Dictionary Online, s.v. "travel."

Chapter Five

1 Peter Hallward, *Damming the Flood: Haiti and the Politics of Containment* (New York: Verso, 2010), 14.

2 Stephanie Hanes, "Jean-Claude Duvalier, Ex-Haitian Leader Known as Baby Doc, Dies at 63," *Washington Post*, October 6, 2014, www.washingtonpost.com.

3 Hallward, *Damming the Flood*, xxiv.

4 Gustavo Gutiérrez, Caridad Inda, and John

Eagleson, *A Theology of Liberation History, Politics, and Salvation* (Maryknoll, NY: Orbis Books, 2014), xxxi.

5 Hallward, *Damming the Flood*, 32.

6 Ibid., 348.

7 Ibid., 33.

8 Dany Laferrière and David Homel, *The World Is Moving around Me: A Memoir of the Haiti Earthquake* (Vancouver: Arsenal Pulp, 2013), 130–31.

9 Hallward, *Damming the Flood*, 33.

10 Ibid.

11 Ibid.

12 Susan Sontag, *Regarding the Pain of Others* (New York: Picador, 2003), 102.

13 Joel Dreyfuss, "Haiti in U.S. History: A Timeline," *The Root*, March 31, 2010, www.theroot.com.

14 Ibid.

15 Ibid.

16 Ibid.

17 Hallward, *Damming the Flood*, 33.

18 Jean-Bertrand Aristide, *An Autobiography* (Maryknoll, NY: Orbis Books, 1993).

19 US Department of State, "A Guide to the United States' History of Recognition, Diplomatic, and Consular Relations, by Country, since 1776: Haiti," n.d., http://history.state.gov/countries/haiti.

20 Vanessa Buschschluter, "The Long History of Troubled Ties between Haiti and the US," BBC News, January 16, 2010, http://news.bbc.co.uk.

21 Ibid.

22 Dreyfuss, "Haiti in U.S. History."

23 Frederick Douglass, "Lecture on Haiti," delivered at the World's Fair, Chicago, January 2, 1893, http://faculty.webster.edu/corbetre/haiti/history/1844-1915/douglass.htm.

24 Hallward, *Damming the Flood*, 37.

25 Sontag, *Regarding the Pain of Others*, 102.

26 Gustavo Gutiérrez, *The Power of the Poor in History* (Maryknoll, NY: Orbis Books, 1983).

27 Hallward, *Damming the Flood*, 35–36.

28 Buschschluter, "Long History of Troubled Ties."

29 Ibid.

30 Ibid.

31 Hallward, *Damming the Flood*, 38.

Chapter Six

1 Francis Fukuyama, "Second Thoughts," *National Interest* (Summer 1989), http://nationalinterest.org.

2 *Stanford Encyclopedia of Philosophy*, "Hegel's Dialectics," by Julie E. Maybee, June 3, 2016, http://plato.stanford.edu.

3 Médecins Sans Frontières, *International Activity Report 2016* (Paris: Médecins Sans Frontières, 2017), www.msf.org.

4 Health Alliance International, "The NGO Code of Conduct," 2008, http://ngocodeofconduct.org.

Chapter Seven

1 Maura R. O'Connor, "Two Years Later, Haitian Earthquake Death Toll in Dispute," *Columbia Journalism Review*, January 12, 2012, http://archives.cjr.org.

2 Centers for Disease Control and Prevention (CDC), "Post-Earthquake Injuries Treated at a Field Hospital— Haiti, 2010," January 07, 2011, www.cdc.gov.

3 Sontag, *Regarding the Pain of Others*, 98.

4 Ibid., 42.

Chapter Eight

1 Clammer, Grosberg, and Raub, *Lonely Planet Dominican Republic and Haiti*, 323.

2 Pan-American Union, *Visit Haiti*, 5.

3 PBS, "Jean Baptiste Lamarck," n.d., www.pbs.org/wgbh/evolution/library/02/3/l_023_01.html.

4 Rudyard Kipling, *The Jungle Book* (New York: Tor, 1988); Rudyard Kipling, *From Sea to Sea and other Sketches: Letters of Travel* (London: Macmillan, 1900).

5 Hallward, *Damming the Flood*, 10.

6 Lorelle Semley, "To Live and Die, Free and French: Toussaint Louverture's 1801 Constitution and the Original Challenge of Black Citizenship," *Radical History Review* (2013): 65, http://www.academia.edu/3736798.

7 Semley, "To Live and Die."

8 Women Suffrage and Beyond, "The Women Suffrage Timeline," last modified 2017, http://womensuffrage.org.

9 Semley, "To Live and Die."

10 Hallward, *Damming the Flood*, 10.

11 Ibid., 11.

12 *History of Boone County, Missouri*. St. Louis: Western Historical Company, 1882.

13 Noland Walker (dir.), *Égalité for All*, documentary film

(San Francisco: Independent Television Service, 2009), http://itvs.org/films/egalite-for-all.

14 Hallward, *Damming the Flood*, 11.

15 Redpath, *Guide to Hayti*, 18.

16 Hallward, *Damming the Flood*, 12.

17 Ibid.

18 Ibid.

19 Jacqueline Charles, "Aristide Pushes for Restitution from France," *Miami Herald*, December 18, 2003, www.latinamericanstudies.org/haiti/haiti-restitution.htm.

20 Charles, "Aristide Pushes for Restitution."

21 Paul Farmer, *The Uses of Haiti*, 3rd ed. (Monroe, ME: Common Courage Press, 2006), 77.

22 Hallward, *Damming the Flood*, 12.

23 Ibid.

24 Pan-American Union, *Visit Haiti*, 6.

25 Charles, "Aristide Pushes for Restitution."

Chapter Nine

1 Mayo Clinic, "Functions of Water in the Body," n.d., www.mayoclinic.org.

2 US Geological Survey, "The Water in You," last modified December 2, 2016, http://water.usgs.gov.

3 CDC, "Chagas Disease," June 2, 2014, www.cdc.gov.

4 Ibid.

5 Richard Knox, "Activists Sue U.N. over Cholera That Killed Thousands in Haiti," National Public Radio, October 09, 2013, www.npr.org.

6 Katz, *Big Truck That Went By*, 228–29.

[7] Susan Sontag, *Illness as Metaphor; and, AIDS and Its Metaphors* (New York: Anchor Books, 1990), 37.

[8] John Eligon, "A Question of Environmental Racism in Flint," *New York Times*, January 21, 2016, www.nytimes.com.

[9] Katz, *Big Truck That Went By*, 232.

[10] US Geological Survey, "Water in You."

[11] CDC, "Chagas Disease."

[12] Katz, *Big Truck That Went By*, 230.

[13] Ed Pilkington and Joe Sandler Clarke, "UN Could Have Prevented Haiti Cholera Epidemic with $2,000 Health Kit—Study," *The Guardian*, April 14, 2016, www.theguardian.com.

[14] Katz, *Big Truck That Went By*, 242.

[15] Rick Gladstone, "After Bringing Cholera to Haiti, U.N. Can't Raise Money to Fight It," *New York Times*, March 19, 2017, www.nytimes.com.

[16] Reuters, "UN Admits 'Involvement' in Bringing Cholera Epidemic to Haiti," *Newsweek*, August 19, 2016, www.newsweek.com.

[17] Gladstone, "After Bringing Cholera to Haiti."

[18] "U.N. Accepts Blame but Dodges the Bill in Haiti," editorial, *New York Times*, March 21, 2017, www.nytimes.com.

[19] *New York Times*, "U.N. Accepts Blame."

Chapter Ten

[1] John McLaughlin, "Woody and Herbaceous Plants Native to Haiti," University of Florida,

http://miami-dade.ifas.ufl.edu/pdfs/urban_hort/
Woody%20and%20Herbaceous%20Plants%20
Native%20to%20Haiti.pdf.

2 Katz, *Big Truck That Went By*, 47.

3 Alex Keksei and Darrel Williams, "Haitian
Deforestation," NASA Scientific Visualization Studio,
October 25, 2002, http://svs.gsfc.nasa.gov/2640.

4 Katz, *Big Truck That Went By*, 56.

Chapter Eleven

1 Oxford English Dictionary Online, s.v. "compassion."

Chapter Thirteen

1 Jean Gardy Marius, "Helping Haiti Help Itself Leads
to Independence from Agencies and Humanitarian
Aid Organizations," OSAPO Haiti, June 4, 2017, http://
osapohaitiblog.wordpress.com.

2 Ibid.

Acknowledgments

To learn more about Maison de Naissance, now known as Global Birthing Home Foundation, please visit globalbirthinghomefoundation.org.

You can find Organizasyon Sante Popilè, or OSAPO, at osapohaitiblog.wordpress.com.

This book began over a decade ago, and the many people who have helped inform the journey and the work since are nearly innumerable. Thank you to my partner, B: you have championed this book from the beginning—and been here for every twist and turn. I am so grateful to my family, Mom, Dad, and Pal, for the love and support these years. And I am so grateful to my many friends, who have led me, followed me, been with me, read drafts, walked miles, spent hours, written in the margins, offered counsel, and of course laughed. My teachers, of which there are many, were my guideposts and buoys: thank you. Thank you to my friends at True/False who were so supportive in the final push of this work.

I'm privileged by the long lineage of nonfiction and the works that helped me dive deeper.

Thank you to Christine, Amanda, and Feliza at

Lanternfish for doing more than believing in this book—thank you for working on it.

For the generosity of spirit of those who made that trip in 2013 possible, I am forever in your debt. Thank you for sharing your knowledge and your stories: Gardy, Sandra, Louna, Rozambert, Kirsty, Mackenzie, Jim, Carine, and everyone who spoke with me. I hope I have done you well.

About the Author

Allison Coffelt lives and writes in Columbia, Missouri. Her work has appeared in the Los Angeles Review of Books, Hippocampus, Oxford Public Health Magazine, the Crab Orchard Review, and elsewhere. She was a finalist for the 2015 Crab Orchard Review Literary Nonfiction Prize and the winner of the 2015 University of Missouri Essay Prize. She currently works as the director of education and outreach for the annual True/False Film Fest and hosts the True/False podcast.